Get Started in Shares

PEARSON

At Pearson, we believe in learning – all kinds of learning for all kinds of people. Whether it's at home, in the classroom or in the workplace, learning is the key to improving our life chances.

That's why we're working with leading authors to bring you the latest thinking and the best practices, so you can get better at the things that are important to you. You can learn on the page or on the move, and with content that's always crafted to help you understand quickly and apply what you've learned.

If you want to upgrade your personal skills or accelerate your career, become a more effective leader or more powerful communicator, discover new opportunities or simply find more inspiration, we can help you make progress in your work and life.

Pearson is the world's leading learning company. Our portfolio includes the Financial Times, Penguin, Dorling Kindersley, and our educational business, Pearson International.

Every day our work helps learning flourish, and wherever learning flourishes, so do people.

To learn more please visit us at: **www.pearson.com/uk**

Get Started in Shares

Trading for the first-time investor

Glen C. Arnold

Harlow, England • London • New York • Boston • San Francisco • Toronto • Sydney • Auckland • Singapore • Hong Kong
Tokyo • Seoul • Taipei • New Delhi • Cape Town • São Paulo • Mexico City • Madrid • Amsterdam • Munich • Paris • Milan

PEARSON EDUCATION LIMITED

Edinburgh Gate
Harlow CM20 2JE
United Kingdom
Tel: +44 (0)1279 623623
Web: www.pearson.com/uk

First published 2013 (print and electronic)

Pearson Education is not responsible for the content of third-party internet sites.

ISBN: 978–0–273–77122–7 (print)
        978–0–273–77834–9 (PDF)
        978–0–273–77833–2 (ePub)

British Library Cataloguing-in-Publication Data
A catalogue record for the print edition is available from the British Library

Library of Congress Cataloging-in-Publication Data
Arnold, Glen.
    Get started in shares : trading for the first-time investor / Glen C. Arnold.
      p. cm.
    Includes index.
    ISBN 978-0-273-77122-7 (pbk.) -- ISBN 978-0-273-77834-9 (PDF) --
ISBN 978-0-273-77833-2 (ePub) 1. Stocks. 2. Investments. 3. Investment
analysis. 4. Portfolio management. I. Title.
    HG4661.A68 2013
    332.63'22-dc23
                            2012043538

The Financial Times. With a worldwide network of highly respected journalists, *The Financial Times* provides global business news, insightful opinion and expert analysis of business, finance and politics. With over 500 journalists reporting from 50 countries worldwide, our in-depth coverage of international news is objectively reported and analysed from an independent, global perspective. To find out more, visit www.ft.com/pearsonoffer.

10 9 8 7 6 5 4 3 2
17 16 15 14 13

Cover design by Dan Mogford
Print edition typeset in 9pt Stone Serif by 3
Print edition printed and bound in Great Britain by Henry Ling Ltd., at the Dorset Press, Dorchester, Dorset

NOTE THAT ANY PAGE CROSS REFERENCES REFER TO THE PRINT EDITION

To Susan Henton, my assistant, whose thoughtful, careful research and qualities as a writer have been of great benefit to me.

Contents

Acknowledgements

To my editor, Christopher Cudmore, at Pearson, who not only encouraged me to write this book but took the time to read and improve draft chapters. His suggestions have made for a much better reading experience. Both you, the reader, and I should be grateful to him for the increased clarity he has brought.

The production team at Pearson did a great job of turning a raw manuscript into the book. I would like to thank Helen MacFadyen and Melanie Carter.

Publisher's acknowledgements

We are grateful to the following for permission to reproduce copyright material:

Figures 1.1, 1.2, 1.3, 1.5 and 7.19 courtesy of MoneyAM Limited; Figures 1.4 and 16.2 reprinted with permission from Yahoo! Inc. 2012 Yahoo! Inc. YAHOO! and the YAHOO! logo are trademarks of Yahoo! Inc.; Figure 2.1 courtesy of Westfries Archief, Hoorn; Figures 5.1, 7.2, 7.3, 7.4, 7.5, 7.6, 7.7, 7.8, 7.9, 7.10, 7.11, 7.12, 7.13, 7.14, 7.15, 7.16, 7.17 and 7.18 courtesy of ADVFN (*www.advfn.com*); Figure 7.1 courtesy of Rolls-Royce plc.

Table 1.2 courtesy of Barclays Capital; Tables 3.3 and 16.1 © The Financial Times Limited. All rights reserved.

Figure 10.1 is based on Porter, M. E., *Competitive Strategy: Techniques for Analyzing Industries and Competitors* (Free Press, 2004), reprinted with the permission of The Free Press, a Division of Simon & Schuster, Inc. Copyright © 2004 by M. E. Porter. All rights reserved.

In some instances we have been unable to trace the owners of copyright material, and we would appreciate any information that would enable us to do so.

About the author

Glen C. Arnold, PhD, has held positions of Professor of Investment and Professor of Corporate Finance, but concluded that academic life was not nearly as much fun as making money in the financial markets. As a wealthy investor in his early 50s Glen now spends most of his time running his own equity portfolio and a small property development company from his office in the heart of rural Leicestershire.

His main research focus explores the questions: 'What works in investment?' drawing on the work of the great investors, academic discoveries and corporate strategic analysis. He is happy to share his ideas with fellow enthusiasts in the City, such as at Schroders Investment Management, where he teaches 20 days each year. He also organises seminar days for private investors to discuss investment philosophies, company analysis and techniques allowing high returns (see his website if you would like to join in).

He authored the best-selling investment books *The Financial Times Guide to Investing* and *The Great Investors*, and wrote *The Financial Times Guide to Value Investing*, which explores the investment philosophies of great investors, and synthesises these with corporate strategic analysis and finance theory into the Valuegrowth Investing framework.

He also wrote the best-selling university textbook *Corporate Financial Management* and the textbooks *Modern Financial Markets and Institutions* and *Essentials of Corporate Financial Management*. *The Financial Times Handbook of Corporate Finance* and *The Financial Times Guide to Financial Markets* also sell well.

List of acronyms

ABI	Association of British Insurers
AGM	annual general meeting
AIM	Alternative Investment Market
AT	automatic trade
CEO	chief executive officer
CGT	capital gains tax
DJIA	Dow Jones Industrial Average
DMA	direct market access
dps	dividend per share
EGM	extraordinary general meeting
EIS	Enterprise Investment Scheme
eps	earnings per share
FCA	Financial Conduct Authority
FOS	Financial Ombudsman Scheme
FPC	Financial Policy Committee
FSA	Financial Services Authority
FSCS	Financial Services Compensation Scheme
GDP	gross domestic product
HMRC	Her Majesty's Revenue and Customs
IPO	initial public offering

ISA	individual savings account
KPI	key performance indicator
LSE	London Stock Exchange
MPC	Monetary Policy Committee
NAV	net asset value
NIM	new issue market
NMS	normal market size
NYSE	New York Stock Exchange
OFR	operating and financial review
PAL	Provisional Allotment Letter
PBIT	profit before interest and tax
PER/PE	price to earnings ratio
PRA	Prudential Regulatory Authority
RIE	recognised investment exchange
ROCE	return on capital employed
ROE	return on equity
SETS	Stock Exchange Electronic Trading System
SFO	Serious Fraud Office
SIPP	self-invested personal pension
TERP	theoretical ex-rights price
UKLA	United Kingdom Listing Authority
VCT	Venture Capital Trust
XD/xd	ex-dividend

Preface

The world of share investing can seem baffling and intimidating. Yet it need not be this way. It really does not require much to make money out of the stock market – just the understanding of a few simple concepts.

Unfortunately jargon hides the commonsense concepts. This book explains the jargon to reveal the fundamental principles of share investing.

I have written it for someone approaching share investment for the first time. It is a simple, straightforward guide to the mysteries of investing, assuming no prior knowledge to build your understanding in a series of easily surmountable steps.

The logical progression in the presentation of concepts, starts with defining what it means to be an owner of shares, how shares allow companies to grow and produce returns for their owners. It then explains how to go about buying shares.

As concisely and clearly as possible this guide cuts through the mystique to explain key issues, such as how

- the stock market works
- you buy and sell shares, and how much it costs
- you compare companies
- you avoid the dangers.

Investing can be fun as well as rewarding. It can certainly earn you much more than you could gain by sticking your money in a bank account. Learn the basics of investing so that you can take control of your finances and grow the wealth of your family.

But you must first learn how to invest in a logical manner with your eyes wide open to the risks as well as the rewards. Learn to be adept at avoiding the traps that catch the unwary investor.

I hope you have as much fun as I have studying the stock market, looking out for bargains, and, of course, enjoying the proceeds.

Happy reading … and happy investing!

Glen C. Arnold

Autumn 2012

The thrill of owning shares

How many millionaires do you know who have become wealthy by investing in savings accounts?

Robert G. Allen

Imagine being the owner of some great companies

You can own a piece of a company. Then over the years it will pay you a portion of the profits it earns as dividends. If that isn't an enticing prospect I don't know what is. Imagine owning a few shares in Rolls-Royce. Every time you see an aeroplane fly overhead you can think to yourself there is a good chance (40% actually) that the engines are made by MY company; and that when the engines are sold or serviced I will reap some of the profit.

Or imagine owning some of Marks & Spencer and walking into the store. You can see the busy tills being filled with money. All so that profits can be paid out in dividends. Day after day you can have the thrill of thinking that sales made by **your** companies are generating **your** future wealth.

Once you have a portfolio, you might look at the garage forecourts of BP slightly differently, as you observe them making money for you. Similarly McDonalds is seen as one of your nest eggs and you start to take a keen interest in the success of the new menus. Even when at play with your children you can enjoy Hornby trainsets, Scalextric and Airfix (all owned by Hornby plc) and wonder how many other families are buying the toys thereby making money for you.

The rewards for being an owner of a company (even if only a part-owner)

So how rewarding would it have been to invest in the companies I have mentioned so far? And would you have done better keeping your money in a bank account?

Let us start with Rolls-Royce. In addition to supplying around 40% of the world's commercial jet engines it also produces engines for ships, fighter aircraft and for shifting natural gas (the car bit was separated off decades ago). I'm writing this in 2012 so let us see how you would have done if you had bought Rolls-Royce shares 10 years previously, when the price of each share back was about £1 to £1.50. First you would have received some dividends. In the first year, 2002, you would have got 8.18p per share. Not bad for an investment of £1 – certainly better than a building society account (offering 3.4% in 2002).

(A *dividend* is simply a payment from the company to each shareholder. Say a company makes profits after tax has been taken of £1m, and it has one million shares issued to its owners, it might pay half of that as dividends to the shareholders equally, i.e. 50p per share. So if you own 1% of the shares (10,000) you will receive £5,000 that year as a dividend.)

That was a good start, but it gets better. In the second year, you would have received another 8.18p. This was followed by annual dividends of 8.18p (2004), 8.72p (2005), 9.59p (2006), 13p (2007), 14.3p (2008), 15p (2009), 16p (2010) and 17.5p (2011). So, ten years of dividends amounted to more than the amount paid for the shares in the first place!

On top of that you would still own a proportion of Rolls-Royce's future profits and future dividends. By this time, other investors in the market place were so enthusiastic about the future prospects of Rolls-Royce that they were willing to pay over £8 for each share.

What a great choice it was to invest in this company. You have received back in dividends all that you put in and then you still have an asset worth eight times the cash devoted in the first place! It wasn't all plain sailing through the ten years though – see the chart of Rolls-Royce's share price over the decade in Figure 1.1 – but it was definitely worth the ups and downs.

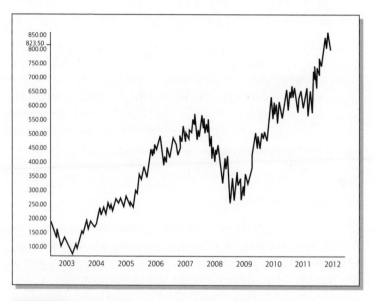

Figure 1.1 Rolls-Royce share price to 2012 (pence per share)

Source: MoneyAM Limited

What about Marks and Spencer? You could have purchased these shares for about £3.50 in 2002. In the next year you would have picked up 9.5p in dividends on each share, followed by a total of 138.7p over the next nine years. The share price rallied strongly until the start of the recession, but ended the 10 years at roughly the place where it started (Figure 1.2) so the overall return is not as great as that for Rolls-Royce. We have to admit that shares are subject to risk – the depth and length of the recession has hit M&S hard, but you would still be ahead over the 10 years, taking into account the dividends.

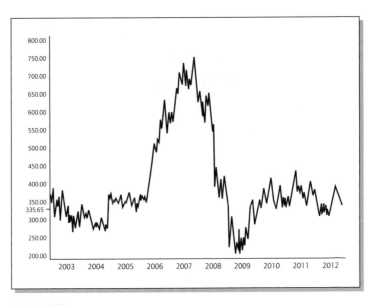

Figure 1.2   Marks and Spencer share price to 2012 (pence per share)

Source: MoneyAM Limited

BP had a major disaster in the Gulf of Mexico in 2009, so it will be interesting to see if it has been a poor investment over the 10 years. You would have paid around 550p per share at the beginning of 2002 which would have fallen to only 417.75p by 2012 (Figure 1.3). Thus, a reduction in the capital amount was experienced. However, the dividends received compensated for this as 200p was paid out over the 10 years.

We have had a bit of a mixed bag so far, large returns and modest returns. This is what it is like with share investing. None of us has a crystal ball to say whether there will be a nasty retail recession around the corner or a massive oil spill. This leads to one of the key lessons in share investing: You must diversify to reduce the impact of one-off events on your overall fund. Of course, by diversifying you must make sure that all your shares are not of the same type, e.g. all oil companies.

Linked to that is the psychological need to stop yourself from getting depressed by focusing too much on one or two invest-

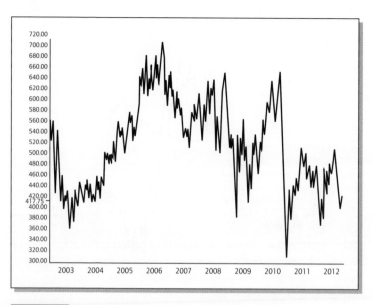

Figure 1.3   BP's share price to 2012 (pence per share)

Source: MoneyAM Limited

ments within the portfolio. You will not get it right every time. The greatest investors ever to have lived reckon they are doing well if they achieve a 55% success rate. This means that they know they will be wrong at least 45% of the time. You have to prepare yourself for this kind of failure rate. If you can be resilient in the face of it then you will, over time, produce a more than satisfactory return.

If you had McDonalds in your portfolio you really would have received a boost. Back in 2002, the shares were priced at around $30. Ten years later they were $100 each (Figure 1.4). On top of that you would have received regular dividends totalling $12.83 over the 10 years. Amazingly, the same shares that are now selling for around $100 were picked up for 35 cents in the early 1970s – a 300-fold rise. And that is before allowing for the dividends which are now over $2.50 per year.

Hornby has had a decade of two halves (Figure 1.5). It was a great success as it transferred production to China in the early noughties, lowering cost without losing quality or image. However, in recent

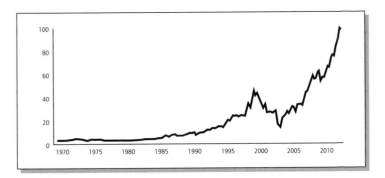

Figure 1.4 McDonald's share price over four decades ($ per share)

Source: Yahoo! Finance UK

years managerial failures in supplying product to stores and in turning leading brands into growing profits mean that its share price has not been the success you might think it would be given the name recognition it has.

Over the decade, the share price rose from around 80p or so to around £3.00 in 2007, but the last five years showed a three-

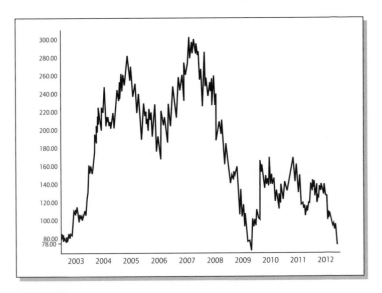

Figure 1.5 Hornby's share price over 10 years (pence per share)

Source: MoneyAM Limited

quarters decline, back to around 78–80p. If only we could see the future and sold out at 300p in 2007!

On the other hand, you would have received handsome dividends over both the first five years (a total of 29.1p) and over the second five years (a total of 29.3p). So, while over the later five years the return is much less than on a savings account at a bank because of the fall in the price of the shares, over 10 years the average annual return is marginally more than on a savings account, with high annual dividends relative to the 80p buy-in price.

How to become a millionaire

This book is definitely not one of those 'get-rich-quick' books, but I will let you into the secret of becoming rich (fairly) slowly with little effort. The sacrifice required is only £100 per month. To make the calculations easier I'll assume the £1,200 saved for the year is invested all in one go at the end of each year.

I'll use real numbers; those based on evidence that we have. The key number you need to know is the average annual return achieved on UK shares over the past 50 years.* This has been 11.3%. This includes dividends and capital gains.

I'm now going to make two assumptions, but I think you'll agree they are not unreasonable ones. First, that the average annual return received by investors over the past 50 years will carry on for another 50. The second is that you will achieve returns on your portfolio equal to the returns achieved on an average UK share portfolio. So, we are not assuming any extraordinary insight or share-picking ability on your part. Merely that you perform as well as the average.

---

* We can get a quick grasp of the two components of 'return' adding up to a 'total return' if we imagine buying a house for £100,000. We rent it out and receive £4,000 for the year, i.e. 4%. On top of that, if we sold it at the end of the year for £110,000 then we make a capital gain of 10%. Thus our 'total return' is 14% for the year. Of course, with shares we get dividends rather than rent.

If you put aside £100 per month over the first year and then invest £1,200 on the last day of the year it will grow to £1,335.60 by the end of the second year at a return rate of 11.3% for the year. At that point you have saved another £1,200 and so you now have £2,535.60 in shares. This will earn 11.3% over the next year to be worth £2,822.12. If you keep doing this, at the end of 10 years the value of your portfolio grows to £20,359.

This is where the thing really starts to take off. We have that eighth wonder of the world working in our favour: 'the power of compound return'. At the end of each year, you not only have the original sums you saved to earn a return in future years (all those £1,200), but you have money credited to your portfolio from past returns – you can earn 'return on the return' for each of the future years.

Compounding is ploughing back the income received and then getting a return on the accumulated ploughed-back money as well as the original capital.

Quite quickly the amount you make on the original sums put in are dwarfed by the return earned on past returns. After 30 years of this discipline, you have over a quarter of a million pounds stashed away. It only takes another 13 years after that to reach the target of £1m – see Figure 1.6.

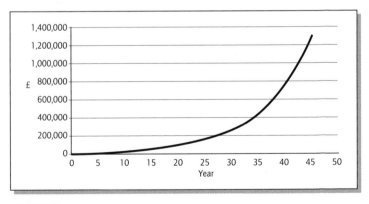

Figure 1.6 The amount in a portfolio at the end of various years if invested at 11.3% per year with £1,200 added each year

Returns over the decades

You might be asking how typical is a return of over 11% p.a.? Is it realistic to expect more or less than this in the future? To help you answer this, I have obtained the returns on UK shares for the whole period 1900 to the beginning of 2012, as well as the returns for each of the decades.† The return numbers in the first column of Table 1.1 are 'real returns' – the return you would have received above inflation. It is interesting that only one decade, 1910–20, showed a negative average annual return. The rest all provided positive returns above inflation.

With inflation added back in (*nominal returns*), we find that since the Second World War there have been many decades with double

Table 1.1 Average annual real rates of return for UK shares (% p.a.) and inflation for the same periods

	Share returns after removing inflation	Average inflation	Nominal return, including inflation
1901–beginning of 2012	4.9	3.9	9
1900–1910	4.0	1.2	5.2
1910–20	−7.9	8.2	0.3
1920–30	12.8	−4.9	7.9
1930–40	2.3	1.1	3.4
1940–50	6.3	1.6	8.0
1950–60	12.1	3.8	16.4
1960–70	3.3	3.5	6.9
1970–80	0.4	12.2	12.7
1980–90	11.7	5.5	17.8
1990–2000	11.8	2.6	14.7
2000–2010	0.6	2.9	3.5

Source: Barclays Capital *Equity Gilt Studies* 2011 and 2012

† I am grateful to Barclays Capital for the use of their numbers (taken from Barclays Capital *Equity Gilt Studies* 2011 and 2012).

digit share returns. So, where do the terrific returns on shares come from? Is it predominantly from the amount the company gives back to you, the dividends? Or is it via capital gains, the rise in the prices of the company?

Over a single year the returns on equities are largely due to share price movement; dividend income contributes a relatively small amount. However, long-term returns are overwhelmingly due to dividends. For example, if a UK share investor had chosen to spend dividends received on a £100 investment made in 1900 as each year passed, rather than reinvest, by January 2012 capital gains alone take the fund to only £11,808‡ (nominal return). On the other hand, another investor who reinvested dividends over the 112 years would have had a fund worth £1,639,368 (nominal return).

International comparison

Perhaps you are thinking that the UK case is freakishly good, and investments in other countries' companies would have lost you money. You are right to be sceptical. Shares are risky. Indeed, investors in many companies have lost all their money and entire markets have been wiped out, e.g. the Russian exchange after 1917. To put your mind at rest consider the return in the 19 leading countries shown in Figure 1.7. These are real returns for 112 years. Clearly there is a great similarity in the average returns across countries. Despite their dramatically different histories (wars, recessions, depressions, etc.) they all show returns above inflation.

However, it is important to note that the small differences in annual percentage returns shown can compound to large differences in the wealth available to investors at the end of a long period. For example, over 112 years the investment of one unit of local currency in the Belgian equity market in 1900 would have grown by a factor of 14 in real terms, whereas a corresponding investment in Australia would have grown 2,408-fold.

---

‡ Barclays Capital *Equity Gilt Study* 2012. The real value of the fund in 1900s pounds is £160.

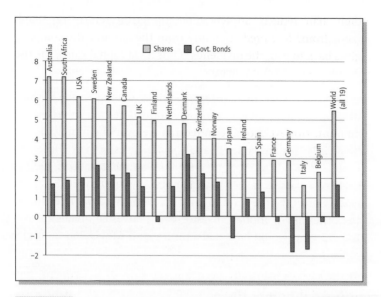

Figure 1.7 Real returns on shares and government bonds, 1900–2011 (% p.a.)

Source: Credit Suisse (2012), Credit Suisse Global Investment Returns Yearbook 2012 (available for internet download)

Comparing the returns on other investments

Also shown in Figure 1.7 are the returns on bonds issued by these governments as they borrow from investors to make up for shortfalls in tax revenues. A bond is a simple way for an organisation to borrow money. Thus a government or company could sell a piece of paper which promises the owner a payment at the end of, say, 10 years as well as a series of interest payments at annual or six-month intervals.

Notice that in all the cases shown in Figure 1.7 you would have been better off invested in shares over the long run. The extra return on shares above government bonds is generally between 3% and 6% per year (over a century or so).

Another alternative investment is to place money in building society accounts. What sort of return would you have got from that strategy? The answer is in Table 1.2 – shares have given much higher returns.

Table 1.2   Building society returns versus UK share returns (average annual nominal)

Decade	Building Society account rate of interest	Share returns
1950s	5.3%	16.4%
1960s	6.5%	6.9%
1970s	10.0%	12.7%
1980s	11%	17.8%
1990s	5.7%	14.7%
2000s	3.5%	3.5%

Source: Barclays Capital *Equity Gilt Study* 2012

So shares have generally been a good form of investment, but there is a downside. They can produce negative real returns for periods as long as a decade (e.g. 1968–78 and 1998–2008). Between 2000 and 2003 UK shares halved in price, as did Japanese shares. German shares fell by two-thirds. They rallied until, in late 2007, they fell again in dramatic fashion. In the 2008 collapse the world index of shares fell by 55%.

It does not take long when looking at statistics like these to form the impression that shares are risky. This is confirmed by Figure 1.8, which shows the real annual returns on UK shares for each year going back to 1900. Over the 112-year period shares produced negative returns in over a third of the years.

Share investors must be able to accept that equity markets can fall by very large percentages during a day and that individual holdings can become worthless overnight as companies go into liquidation. If you are unable to accept this degree of volatility perhaps you should be investing somewhere else. Building society and bank accounts beckon.

For those who are prepared to take some risk then the share markets offer many exciting possibilities. Many investors have become millionaires – some by being lucky and backing the likes of Vodafone, Google or Apple at the right moment, but most

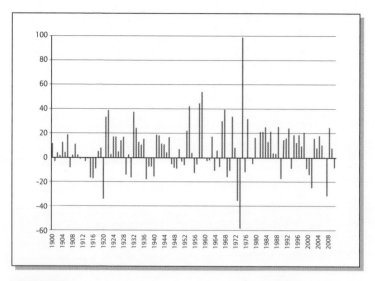

Figure 1.8 UK annual real equity returns, 1900–2011(%)

Source: Barclays Capital *Equity Gilt Study* 2012

by steadily accumulating a portfolio in a disciplined way over a number of years.

Start your exhilarating adventure into the thrills and spills of the stock market now by reading the next few chapters and learning the basics of investment.

2

Businesses and shares

Whenever you see a successful business, someone once made a courageous decision.

Peter F. Drucker

The limited liability corporation is the greatest single invention of modern times.

Columbia University president Nicholas Murray Butler

What is a share?

If you are to start share buying it makes sense to first get the answer to the question, what are shares?

Ordinary shares give the holder the right to claim a share of ownership of the business. If you held all the ordinary shares you would own the company outright and then you will be the only person that the managers of the business are answerable to. You can sack them if you want to. If you hold a small proportion then you have to share the rights of ownership, such as deciding on the team of directors or the size of dividends, with other share-holders. When there are many shareholders companies use voting mechanisms to find out what the majority of shareholders want to happen.

Why do we need shares?

Companies with a large number of shareholders are a relatively recent invention. To understand the importance of this break-through for us all we need to step back and consider some basic problems that people had to solve.

Willingness to take a hit

Society needs people who are willing to take the risk of total failure of a business enterprise. Banks are not willing to accept that risk. They strike deals with companies whereby even if the profits are low or a loss is made they are still paid interest and capital. Also, they usually require *collateral* so that if the business plan turns out to be a dud the bank can recoup its money (or, at least most of its money most of the time) by selling off property or other assets.

Imagine if debt were the only form of capital available for businesses to grow. Very few would be established because it would be rare for managers to come across an investment project (e.g. new product-line, factory) that offered the lenders the security they need. I can only think of one company that is virtually completely financed by debt. This is the water company for Wales. It can get away without many shares (equity) because there is so little uncertainty regarding its future income. It is regulated and the bills it charges to customers are highly predictable for years to come and so it can offer its lenders high security, not just from its cash flow but also from the land, reservoirs, etc. that it owns.

Risk and the television

Consider a company producing television programmes. Could it finance itself entirely with debt? No, because if £100m was put in by lenders to invest in 10 television serials there is nothing for them to fall back on should one-half of the shows be poorly received by viewers. They might be willing to lend, say, £40m if the other £60m came from investors who were willing to accept the risk of total loss.

Then the lenders know that their money is likely to be reasonably safe – assuming that they have faith in the track record of the executives in charge and the historical statistics suggest that only two or three programmes are likely to be commercial flops.

Naturally, the risk takers providing this £60m of capital will want a high reward for putting their hard-earned savings to such an exposure. They would also want the power to vote down major moves proposed by the managers. Furthermore they will insist on receiving regular information on progress. These holders of shares (*equities*) in the success or failure of the enterprise act as shock-absorbers so that other parties contributing to a firm, from suppliers and creditors to bankers and leasing companies, do not have to bear the shock of a surprise recession, a loss of market share to competitors or a badly made TV series.

Redemption and perpetual life

Another attractive feature of share capital for businesses is that it does not have a date at which it will be redeemed by the company. The managers (and creditors) know that the capital will be available for the very long term, that the shareholders cannot turn around one day and demand their money back. That is the deal; if you buy a share from the company it is not obliged to buy it back from you, they hold onto your cash.

However, this causes a problem for investors because they may want to sell their shares a year or two down the line. While many shareholders are willing to accept that their companies are too small to join a stock market or that the disadvantages of doing so outweigh the advantages, a minority of companies have decided to float their shares on an exchange or stock market. This brings many benefits in addition to permitting shareholders to sell (or buy more) when they want to, including facilitating mergers and the raising of more equity finance. We will discuss these later in the book.

The value of joint stock enterprises: a little history

It is in seventeenth-century Europe that the earliest shares were issued and traded, and the first stock exchange was founded in Amsterdam. These shares were in the Vereinigte Oostindische Compagnie (VOC, the Dutch East India Company). The oldest VOC share still in existence (and only discovered in 2010) was issued on 9 September 1606 (see Figure 2.1). The second page records the payments of dividends.

Figure 2.1 World's oldest surviving share certificate

Source: Westfries Archief, Hoorn

The opening of commercial routes to the East saw a huge surge in trading, with groups of merchants pooling their resources to finance voyages in the hope of significant profits. It was simply too much for one supplier of capital to pay for the whole venture. Collective investing, buying shares in a trading company, lessened the individual exposure to risk and there were plenty of wealthy businessmen eager to purchase shares with their promise of returns far in excess of any return offered by banks.

Over in Britain

In the UK, trading in securities began in 1698 when a John Castaing based at Jonathan's Coffee House published a list of stock and commodity prices called 'The Course of the Exchange and other things'. A club formed at Jonathan's Coffee House in 1801 to deal in shares and made up of subscribing members was called the Stock Exchange.

Shares enabled companies to expand to take advantage of the industrial age. They attracted investors to buy equity (a share) in the companies in return for a share in the profits. In the nineteenth century, canal corporations, docks companies, manufacturing enterprises, railways, mining, brewing and insurance companies were added to the list of firms with shares and bonds traded on the stock exchanges of Europe, America and a few places in Asia.

Partnerships and liability

Partnerships

If a few friends have a great idea for a new business, one option is to form a *partnership*. Say there are 10 investors each willing to supply some of the money. Perhaps only one would have the time to work full-time in the business. The others would supply funds only, they would be *sleeping partners*. The profits would be split in proportion to the finance supplied except for the one who takes on a full-time managerial role; he or she would be entitled to an extra income.

Partnerships are a good form of organisation for many businesses and there are millions of successful partnerships ranging from John Lewis down to husband and wife corner shops. However, there are two difficulties with partnerships, which are particularly bothersome if hundreds of strangers, or even 10 friends, are each contributing ownership capital to establish and expand a business.

1   Each partner is liable for the debts of the business. Thus each partner has to accept that if the business incurs liabilities and it cannot satisfy the creditors then they can come after their personal assets, houses, farms, etc.

2   If one of the partners wishes to leave (or dies) then he/
she is generally entitled to a fair share of the value of the
partnership. This can be very disruptive to the business, as
assets have to be sold to pay the partner. Indeed, partnerships
tend to be dissolved if one member leaves, and then a new
partnership is created to carry on the business.

Organisations as 'separate persons'

To solve these two problems, financial markets developed the idea
of a company or corporation established as a 'separate person'
under the law. It is the company that enters legal agreements such
as bank loan contracts, not the owners of the company shares. The
company can have a *perpetual life*. So, if an investor wishes to cash
in his or her holding they do not have the right to insist that the
company liquidate its assets to pay them their share. The company
continues, but the investor sells his or her share in the company to
another investor.

This is great – it gives managers the opportunity to plan ahead,
knowing the resources of the business will not be withdrawn; it
gives other shareholders the reassurance that the company can
achieve its goals without disruption.

Limited versus unlimited

One of the most important breakthroughs in the development
of capitalism and economic progress was the introduction of
limited liability (1855 in the UK). There were strong voices heard
against the change in the law. It was argued that it was only
fair that creditors to a business could call on the shareholders
in that business to bear the responsibility of failure. However,
a stronger argument triumphed. This is that it is better for
society as a whole if we encourage individuals to place their
savings at the disposal of entrepreneurial managers for use in
a business enterprise. Thus factories, ships, shops, houses and
railways will be built and society will have more goods and
services.

Insisting on *un*limited liability for investors made them hesitant to invest and thus reduced overall wealth. Limited liability companies are what (for the most part) we have today, and we should be very grateful for it. Creditors quickly adjusted to the new reality of lending without a guarantee other than from the company. They became more expert and thorough in assessing the risk of the loan going bad and they called for more information; legislators helped by insisting that companies publish key information.

Directors are not the same as owners

With many smaller companies (e.g. a husband and wife team) the owners of the shares are also the directors. However, the two roles are legally distinct. You can be a shareholder without being a director; and a director without being a shareholder.

Those companies with shares available for purchase on a stock exchange are usually run by a team of directors – rarely less than five individuals, often many more. The directors divide into two types. Both are (or should be) concerned with acting in the best interests of all the shareholders jointly, but the *executive directors* deal with the day-to-day running of the business.

The *non-executive directors* are selected by the shareholders to advise the board on strategic and other vital actions, and to make sure that the executive directors and other managers are doing a good job for the shareholders (the *stewardship* role). They are there to set standards for the managers and to then periodically judge their performance.

The non-execs are meant to be business-savvy experts. Crucially, they are expected to be (or are supposed to be – some are not!) independent of the favours of the executive team so that they can exercise judgement without fear or favour when examining the performance and plans of the executives. For example, non-executives should not be dependent on the income they receive for the few days a year they devote to Board of Director meetings and other company matters.

The *chairman* is usually a non-executive whose role is to run the board of directors (chairing meetings so that all have a chance of a fair say, helping selecting/sacking directors, prompting strategic discussion, setting the agenda, etc.). This might involve more work than for the other non-execs, say one or two days a week rather than one or two per month.

In quite a number of cases, the chairman works as an executive in a full-time capacity and often dominates both the day-to-day business operations and the running of the board. This is not regarded as best practice by investors because it is better to have the executive role in the hands of one person and the board leadership in the hands of another to avoid excessive power in the hands of one individual.

In reality many chairmen and other non-execs are far too pally with the chief executive officer (CEO)* and other executive directors, often failing to hold them to account either out of laziness, ignorance or sense of obligation to those who appointed them to a position where they can take home more than the average wage for 10–20 days of work per year. As Warren Buffett, the great investor, ruefully puts it, 'Relations between the Board and the CEO are expected to be congenial. At board meetings, criticism of the CEO's performance is often viewed as the social equivalent of belching. No such inhibitions restrain the office manager from critically evaluating the substandard typist.'†

Not all boards of directors are this bad. Many have very competent and highly experienced tough-minded business men and women with specialist knowledge to offer keeping a beady eye on the hired hands, such as the finance director and chief executive. But we only have to think back to the bank crisis of 2008 to realise that

---

* The CEO or chief executive is the most important leader. In the old days they were usually referred to as Managing Director. Indeed, in many companies they still have that title. However, increasingly we are following American titling so CEO is taking over.

† Buffett, W.E. (1988) Letter to shareholders included with the 1988 Annual Report of Berkshire Hathaway Inc. www.berkshirehathaway.com. Copyrighted material reprinted with the permission of the author.

all too often non-execs can fall asleep on the job and blindly trust that operations are being run well and at low risk.

Some more on ordinary shares

You know now that ordinary shares represent the equity capital of a firm and are a means of raising long-term finance to run the business. While some companies issue other types of shares (see Chapter 8) the vast majority of shares issued by companies are ordinary, which carry a special set of legal rights. Ordinary shareholders have a claim to a share of the company's profits in the form of dividend payments. These are not automatic. They are paid only if the company has been successful enough to pay dividends and the company decides to pay them. In addition, in a worst-case scenario, the ordinary shareholders have a right to share in the proceeds of a liquidation sale of the firm's assets, albeit after all other creditors such as banks, tax authorities, trade creditors, etc. have been paid.

Significantly, one of the rights they do not carry is a guarantee of any return on the money handed over to buy the ordinary shares. Any return for the holders of these securities lies in the (hopefully) rising prosperity of a company.

Reports and payouts

Shareholders of stock market quoted companies have the right to receive an *annual report and accounts* and an *interim report and accounts* (half year) detailing their financial performance and financial position (amount of debt, etc.). They also have the right to attend an annual meeting (*Annual General Meeting, AGM*‡) where they can question the directors on their handling of the business as well vote on, say, a merger proposal, the raising of more capital by selling some more shares, or the election of directors.

---

‡ Shareholders owning more than 10% of the ordinary shares (10% of voting rights) can also insist on another meeting of the company, i.e. shareholders and directors, being convened. This is termed an *extraordinary general meeting* (EGM). These EGMs may also be convened when the directors think fit.

Annual, semi-annual or quarterly dividend payments are paid at the discretion of the directors, and individual shareholders are often effectively powerless to influence the income from a share because of the relative power of directors in a firm with a disparate or divided shareholder body. If a shareholder owns 100 shares of a company with millions of shares in issue, there is little likelihood of this person exerting any influence at all; institutional shareholders, such as large pension funds, who often control very large amounts of shares are able to bring more pressure to bear.

Stocks and shares

There is some lack of clarity on the distinction between stocks and shares. Shares are equities in companies, i.e. an ownership share of the business representing an equal stake in the business. This is the 'risk capital' as described above. Stocks are financial instruments that pay interest, e.g. bonds. However, in the USA shares are also called *common stocks* and the shareholders are often referred to as stockholders. So when some people use the term stocks they could be referring to either bonds or shares.

Being British I'll try to hold back the tide of Americanisms (Canute-like, I hear you saying) and stick with calling shares shares – despite the fact that an increasing proportion of *Financial Times* writers are calling them stocks and refer to the equity capital providers as *stockholders*. Trans-Atlanticism gone too far!

It's easy to create shares

I have done it many times – create shares out of thin air, that is. Once a company is set up with its constitution (Articles of Association and Memorandum of Association – just a set of rules binding on the shareholders and directors) and been registered with Companies House down in Cardiff – a process that takes an hour or two of form filling, a few days for bureaucratic wheels to turn and a few dozen pounds – it is free to issue more shares if the existing shareholders approve of this.

Creating shares in a small company

In later years, the shareholders of a small company (who are usually also directors) simply need to call a 'meeting', say, while having a coffee, and agree to create more shares and issue these to themselves or outsiders in exchange for, say, 10p per share. Then it is off to the computer to write the minutes of the shareholders' and directors' meetings and to alter the share ownership record. If the owner of the new shares would like it, a fancy-looking certificate can be created and handed over, but this is not necessary. If the company is growing fast and needs more equity capital they can call numerous meetings during the year to sell additional shares.

A few weeks after issuing the shares Companies House is informed of the injection of fresh capital and the issuance of new shares. This information is then accessible to all if they just visit the website of Companies House and pay a pound or two to look at the records of a company (a visitor can also see the annual accounts and other information about the company).

What about share creation in large firms?

When it comes to companies on stock markets with thousands of shareholders, the process is essentially the same in that shareholders have strong powers to approve the creation and issue of shares. However, when the shareholders are numerous and the directors are not the same people as the shareholders we need much stronger safeguards to protect *minority shareholders*. These are investors with a small percentage of the voting rights who could be exploited by the large holders acting against their interests, e.g. the dominant shareholders vote to issue millions of shares at a discounted price to their relatives. We will look at many of the restrictions in later chapters, particularly when it comes to selling shares to outsiders when the company first joins a stock exchange (Chapter 14) and when it subsequently issues more shares (Chapter 15).

Authorised, issued and par values

When a company is created, the original shareholders will decide the number of shares to be authorised (the *authorised capital*). This is the maximum amount of share capital that the company can issue (unless shareholders subsequently vote to change the limit). In many cases, firms do not issue up to the amount specified.

For example, Green plc has authorised capital of £4m of ordinary shares. However, the company has not issued all the ordinary shares that its shareholders have given permission to be created. The issued ordinary share capital stands at only £2.5m, leaving £1.5m as *authorised but unissued ordinary share capital*. This allows the directors to issue the remaining £1.5m of capital without being required to ask shareholders for further permission (subject to the rights issue or placing rules – see later, in Chapter 15).

You say par, I say nominal

Shares have a stated par value, say 25p or 5p. This nominal value usually bears no relation to the price at which the shares could be sold or their subsequent value. So let us assume Green has 10 million ordinary shares issued, each with a par value of 25p (£2.5m total nominal value divided by the nominal price per share, 25p = 10m shares); these were originally sold for £2 each, raising £20m. However, the present market value is £3.80 per share.

The par value has no real significance§ and for the most part can be ignored. However, a point of confusion can arise when you examine company accounts because issued share capital appears on the balance sheet at par value and so often seems pathetically small. This item has to be read in conjunction with the *share premium account*, which represents the difference between the price received by the company for the shares and the par value of those shares. Thus, in the case of Green the premium on each

---

§ Except that it shows proportional voting and income rights.

share was 200p − 25p = 175p. The total share premium in the balance sheet will be £17.5m.

Two real world examples:

- Rolls-Royce shares have a nominal/par value of 20p but are now selling at over £8. So if the company wanted to sell some more they could do so for a lot more than 20p – of course the shares would have to be created by the shareholders first authorising them.
- The par value of Hornby shares are 1p while selling for around 78p.

Public, private and listed

Private companies, with the suffix 'Limited' or 'Ltd', are the most common form of company (over 95% of all UK companies). The less numerous, but more influential, form of company is a *public limited company* (or just public companies). These firms must display the suffix 'plc'. The private company has no minimum amount of share capital and there are restrictions on the type of purchaser who can be offered shares in the enterprise, whereas the plc has to have a minimum share capital of £50,000 but is able to offer shares to a wide range of potential investors.

Not all public companies are quoted on a stock market; in fact, most are not. This can be particularly confusing when the press talks about a firm 'going public' – it may have been a public limited company for years and has merely decided to 'come to the market' to obtain a quotation.

Strictly speaking, the term *listed* should only be applied to those firms on the Official List (i.e. those accepted by the UK Listing Authority – most of which are on the Main Market of the London Stock Exchange), but the term is used rather loosely and shares on other markets are often referred to as being quoted or listed.

No right to vote

To this point we have assumed that a company issues only one type of ordinary share; and each of these has equal powers – the equity holders are equally ranked. However *non-voting shares* or *reduced voting shares* are sometimes issued by family-controlled firms which need additional equity finance but wish to avoid the diluting effects of an ordinary share issue. These shares are often called *'A' shares* or *'B' shares* (or *N/V*) and usually get the same dividends, and the same share of assets in a liquidation, as the ordinary shares.

The issue of non-voting or reduced voting shares is contentious, with many investors saying that everyone who puts equity into a company should have a vote on how that money is spent: the 'one share one vote' principle. On the other hand, investors can buy 'non-voters' for less than 'voters' and thereby gain a higher rate of return. Also, without the possibility of issuing non-voting shares, many companies would simply prefer to forgo expansion. They want capital to grow but they want freedom from interference even more.

Around one-third of Europe's largest businesses fail to observe the one share one vote principle. In the USA, the Ford family own a mere 3.75% of the shares. However, when the motor company joined the New York Stock Exchange in 1956 the family's shares were converted into a special class that guaranteed 40% of the voting power, no matter how many ordinary shares are in issue. When Google floated in 2004 Larry Page and Sergey Brin, the founders, held 'B' shares each with 10 times as many votes per share as the 'A' shares issued to other investors. Mark Zuckerberg made sure he held 56% of the voting rights in Facebook despite owning a much smaller percentage of the shares because each one of his shares has 10 votes compared to one vote for the 'A' shares sold to the general public in 2012.

In the UK, there are very few companies with reduced voting rights, but it is something you need to watch out for.

Parents and groups

Companies can own companies. That is, they can buy all or some of the shares in other companies. Most of the firms in which you might hold shares will control many other companies. Usually they own 100% of the shares, but it might be they have 50% or 60%. This is often enough to decide who will be the directors and other important matters.

Being subject to this level of control makes the firm concerned a *subsidiary* of the parent firm. This means that when the accounts are drawn up to show profit or balance sheet assets, etc. there are accounts for each of the 'separate persons', i.e. each of the companies and, in addition there is a set of accounts for the '*group*'. For the group accounts the entire income, costs, property values, etc. of each of the subsidiaries are lumped in together with the parent's income, costs, property values, etc. in one consolidated whole (*consolidated accounts*). This happens even if the parent only owns, say, 70% of the shares of a subsidiary. The accountants allow for the fact that 30% of the subsidiary's profits and asset values are owned by other shareholders in a separate entry in the accounts (*minority interests* or *non-controlling interests*).

Thus the accounts you need to look at when examining a company to see whether you might want to invest are the group accounts or consolidated accounts, which include all the different companies combined.

Primary versus secondary markets

The final pieces of jargon we need to deal with in this chapter are primary markets and secondary markets.

Primary market

The primary market is when shares, bonds or other financial instruments are issued for the first time and sold directly to investors. When a company sells its shares on a regulated exchange for the first time, this is known as the *new issue market* (*NIM*). The most common issue in the primary market is the *initial public offering (IPO)*. When it is shares that are sold this is known as a *flotation*, where they are offered for sale to the public in new, young companies or well-established private companies, wishing to obtain funding for their company in the form of equity capital.

Companies already listed on a stock exchange can also raise capital in the primary market by issuing, say, a *rights issue* – issuing further shares in their company to their current shareholders (see Chapter 15).

Secondary market

Secondary trading is the buying and selling of securities between investors (the company does not receive the value of the sale; a selling investor does). The existence of the secondary market is clearly a positive factor for potential investors in a company raising money in the primary market, and so funds are supplied at a lower cost than if there was no secondary market.

3

What you receive from the company

Whereas companies routinely reward their shareholders with higher dividends, no company in the history of finance, going back as far as the Medicis, has rewarded its bondholders by raising the interest on a bond.

Peter Lynch*

Once you have bought your shares there are three ways of benefiting from them:

- A regular flow of income – dividends
- A rise in price of the shares – capital gain
- Various gifts and discounts from the company – shareholder perks

A flow of cash income

It is a great feeling to open the post one morning and be told that your account has been credited with money or a cheque is in the envelope – certainly better than another bill! Your companies will usually send you such a letter twice a year at six monthly intervals.

---

* *Beating the Street* (1994), Simon and Schuster, p. 50.

The first is called an *interim dividend* or *interim payment* and is sent shortly after the end of the first six months of the company's financial year (this is not the same as the calendar year because companies can choose the date for their year-end). The amount you receive depends on the number of shares you hold because all dividends are on a per-share basis; announced as pence or euro cents per share.

The second payment, *final dividend*,† will arrive a few months after the end of the financial year. First, the preliminary results (profits, etc.) for the year are published a few weeks after the year-end and the dividend amount is proposed by the directors within these. These accounts are like a first draft and are not the official version.

When the final report and accounts are published a month or so later the shareholders are invited to attend the AGM where they are able to vote to approve or reject the dividend proposed in the report by the board of directors (they rarely reject). If they cannot attend they can send in their vote by post. The final dividend then arrives a few days after the AGM. If you add the interim and the final dividend together you have the *total dividend* for the year.

Some companies pay only a final dividend and no interim (due to lower administration costs), others pay no dividend at all for many years. This is often because they need the cash to invest in exciting projects, e.g. Apple did not pay a dividend for many years when it was developing the iPhone and the iPad.

A few UK and European companies pay dividends every quarter – so you get a heart-warming letter every three months! These are mostly companies with large-scale operations in the USA and with a high proportion of US shareholders (e.g. BP). Most US companies pay *quarterly dividends*.

---

† I am grateful to Barclays Capital for the use of their numbers (taken from Barclays Capital *Equity Gilt Studies* 2011 and 2012).

Why is the interim dividend smaller?

There is no regulation about the relative sizes of the interim and final dividends, although companies tend to be cautious by paying an interim that is a small proportion of the total for the year. The interim is usually around one-half that of the final dividend. Reasons:

■ Because the dividends are merely recommended by the directors and are subject to approval by the shareholders at the AGM they might be rejected or revised downwards months after the interim has already been paid. Despite this being extremely rare it is theoretically possible and so to be on the safe side the directors only pay around one-third of the expect annual amount at the half-way stage.

■ Business is a risky activity with unforeseen events causing great damage to the expected profits. It could easily be that the second half is badly hit and the company falls into losses. In these circumstances, the directors might come to regret paying out cash as an interim dividend.

How much is paid?

Companies can choose the level of the dividends they pay. They can pay more than the total of the year's profits after tax if they want, so long as they have accumulated profits from previous years still within the company.‡ Most companies, however, settle in a band of dividend payments which is around 40–60% of that year's annual profits after tax.

Generally, directors bend over backwards to avoid sudden changes in dividends. There are two main reasons for this. First, some investors like to have a predictable income stream from their shares; there are 'clients' for steady dividend payers. The problem

---

‡ They can only pay dividends out of *revenue reserves* which is the stock of previous year's profits that have not yet been paid out plus the gains made when non-current assets ('fixed assets' in old parlance) are sold. This is after deduction of tax on these and netting out any losses made on disposal of non-current assets.

is that profits in many industries can be quite volatile. If the company stuck rigidly to, say, a 50% payout of after-tax profits the dividend too would jump about from one year to the next, upsetting many of their owners.

The second reason is that dividend changes are taken as a signal by investors of the level of confidence directors have in the rising prosperity of the firm. A steadily rising dividend (*a progressive dividend policy*) from one year to the next signals that the company is on an improving trend. When they are hit by temporary bad weather they do not cut the dividend unless they really have to, e.g. they are over-indebted. Likewise, when they have an unusually good year they do not raise the dividend to match the improvement in short-term profits for fear that they might have to cut it again the following year.

Did you mean to send that signal?

Having said this, not all company directors are sensitive to the signalling effect of dividend changes. I once quizzed a chairman at an annual general meeting on whether he meant to signal to the market that his outlook for the firm was gloomy. The dividend was significantly down on the year and, as a consequence, the share price had fallen by half.

He said, 'No, I am optimistic about the future. It is just that we have a policy of paying out one-half of profits after tax as dividends. I have never heard of this signalling idea.' I took this as a miscommunication with the market. Investors heard one thing and the directors meant another. I promptly bought a few thousand more shares in the company. Within the year they had doubled in price as the market realised that the firm was doing fine after all. Sometimes it pays to pop along to the AGM and talk to the key people!

Dividend cover

By maintaining a 50% payout ratio this chairman was targeting a *dividend cover* of 2. That is, profits after tax cover the size of the dividend twice over. Let's say it has 10 million shares in issue and

Table 3.1	Some examples of earnings and dividends					
Company	Profits after tax	Number of shares	Earnings per share	Total dividends	Dividend per share	Dividend cover
Rolls-Royce	£850m	1,875m	45.33p	£328m	17.5p	2.6
M & S	£513m	1,579m	32.5p	£268m	17p	1.9
Hornby	£2.855m	38m	7.5p	£1.9m	5p	1.5

Source: Annual reports of the companies

made £2m profit after tax. Then the *earnings per share* (*eps*) are 20p per share. If £1m is paid as dividends the *dividend per share* (*dps*) is 10p. Some real-world examples are shown in Table 3.1.

Dividend cover highlights the affordability of the current level of dividends. It shows the number of the current dividend payments that could be made out of current after-tax profits. The higher the proportion of profits paid out, the less is available for business investment and growth.

A dividend cover of 3 or more is regarded as being very conservative. Anything below 1.5 is regarded as being suspect, because a modest fall in profits can result in the dividend being larger than the profits, which is obviously unsustainable. The fear is that the dividend might need to be cut.

Switching around the top and bottom of the ratio gives the *payout ratio*. This is the percentage of after-tax profit paid to shareholders in dividends.

When do I get paid?

Companies have a financial calendar, usually available to view on the website, which sets out when dividends will be paid. This will help you find out when you need to be an owner of a share in order to receive a dividend. We will use the case of Marks & Spencer to illustrate – see Table 3.2.

Its year-end is 2 April 2012. So the profits for the previous 12 months are added up and a balance sheet is drawn up for that

Table 3.2   Marks & Spencer's Financial Calendar

11 January 2013	Interim ordinary dividend payment date*
16 November 2012	Record date to be eligible for interim dividend*
14 November 2012	Ex-dividend date – interim dividend*
06 November 2012	Announcement of half year results*
13 July 2012	Final ordinary dividend payment date
10 July 2012	Annual General Meeting
1 June 2012	Record date to be eligible for final dividend
30 May 2012	Ex-dividend date – final dividend
22 May 2012	Announcement of final results

* provisional dates
Source: www.marksandspencer.com

date. This takes time to do and so the company does not announce its results until 22 May. This is remarkably fast; most companies take at least two months. In this announcement there will be a figure proposed as the dividend amount (the final for the year). This was 10.8p per share.

The company does not pay the dividend on this *announcement day* (also called the *declaration day*). Rather it states something like it 'will be paid on 13 July 2012 to shareholders who are on the Register of Members on 1 June 2012'. That may seem like a long time to wait, but there are sound reasons for the delay.

First, the directors need to figure out who is actually a shareholder entitled to receive the dividends. Every working day some holders of shares sell them to new investors and so the list of registered shareholders changes frequently. It is thought best to set a date sometime in the future, which is the day when the share register will be looked at to see who is on it. Those on the list will get dividends. In the case of M&S this date was 1 June 2012.

However, this is not the end of the story, because, remember, the final dividend for the year is merely 'proposed' by the directors. It has to be approved by the shareholders at the AGM. So the payout cannot take place until after the meeting – this is just in case the shareholders decide something different (very unlikely, but it could happen).

So the date of actual payment via direct electronic bank transfer to your account or by receiving a cheque is made a few days after the AGM.

So, you now ask, why are there two dates for dividend eligibility in Table 3.2, one called *Ex-dividend date* and the other the *Record date*? The two are necessary because of the delay in registering you as a new shareholder when you buy a share. There is more on this in Chapter 5, but what you need to know now is that, if you went to your broker and instructed him or her to buy a share today, he or she would *execute* the trade today (on the grisly-sounding 'execution day'), but it usually takes three days to settle the deal. This is when the trade is finished and your name is put on the shareholder register. This is the date you actually pay for the shares and become the owner.

If M&S are intent on looking at the share register on 1 June to check who is eligible for the dividend then they need to warn potential new buyers of shares that there will be a date two days earlier, before which they have to execute the deal to buy the shares to get the dividend. Thus if you buy on the day before it goes ex-dividend you will registered as the shareholder on 1 June 2012. If, however, you purchase on the ex-dividend day, 30 May, you will not be registered until 2 June, which is too late to receive the dividend. The records will show the previous shareholder as the owner and the dividend will flow to him or her.

Note that anyone who is an official shareholder on the record date will receive the dividends on the payment date even if they sell the shares between the date of record and the payment date.

The ex-dividend (also called XD or xd) day is the key date for an investor because buying shares on or after it excludes the possibility of receiving the dividend. Prior to trading ex-dividend the shares will have been labelled *cum-dividend* following the announcement that a dividend will be paid.

Don't worry about sharp share moves on ex-div day

Novice investors can get caught out by the apparent weird movements in share prices on ex-dividend days – they seem to plummet. But that is just the logical consequence of any new buyer losing the right to receive dividend income a few weeks hence.

If a share is currently cum-dividend any buyer today will receive the dividend of, say, 12p in six weeks. The share might therefore be trading at, say, 300p. If the following day it goes ex-dividend and is then sold, the seller will be the person on the share register on the record day and so will receive the dividend. Thus the new buyer will pay around 300p minus 12p for the shares, assuming all else remains constant.

So, do not be panicked into thinking something terrible has happened with your company if its share price drops suddenly – check to see if it has merely gone XD. The financial pages of newspapers show an XD or xd next to the share in the tables.

Downloading data on dividends for a company

One source of information on a company's dividends is to visit its website and examine the reports and accounts going back many years. An alternative is to visit one of the free financial websites where the dividend history is available. Chapter 7 has more on financial websites.

Dividend yield

Beware of falling into the trap of looking for a share that has a large dividend expressed in pence per share. Don't be too quick to be attracted to a company offering say 34p per share rather than one offering 12p – at least not until you have checked out the current share price. What really matters is the dividend as a percentage of the price paid for the share. This is called the *dividend yield*.

If the first company's shares are selling for £9, the dividend yield is 34p divided by 900p, which is 3.78%. If the second company's shares are selling for 120p, the dividend yield is a much more attractive 10%.

Dividend yields can be calculated on *historical* figures (based on the most recent 12 months of dividends) or on a *prospective* basis (also called *future* basis), which makes use of the forecast for dividends for the next year.

Dividend yield is important because it is the near-term cash return you are actually receiving from a company. You may hope to make capital gains as well, but this is somewhat theoretical – dividend income is real.

The dividend yield offered on a share can be compared with the sector it is in, or the market as a whole. Such a comparison may show you if it has an unusually high or low yield. It can also be compared with other investments such as government bonds or building society accounts. In 2012, the average dividend yield at around 4% was about double that on interest-bearing investments. This is very unusual, caused by the pushing down of interest rates in the recession and the simultaneous lowering of share prices (while dividend payouts held up well). Yields on shares are usually significantly less than those on a government bond. This is because shareholders can normally expect a rising dividend in future years, whereas the interest on bonds is usually fixed for the whole life of the bond.

Those companies expected to grow their profits at a fast rate will have low dividend yields because investors tend to bid up the share price. These *lower-yield shares* are often labelled *growth shares*. *Higher-yield* (or simply *yield*) *shares* are expected to have low profits growth and are often labelled *value shares*.§ Shares offering very

---

§ This is a crude definition of 'growth' and 'value' shares and should not be taken too seriously – see Glen Arnold, *The Financial Times Guide to Value Investing* (Financial Times Prentice Hall, 2009) for the poor quality of thinking demonstrated by crudely classifying shares as value or growth. Alternatively, you might like to join us for a day of seminars focused on understanding the investing approaches of great investors such as Warren Buffett – see *www.glen-arnold-investments.co.uk*

high yields often indicate market consensus that the dividend will fall as the company heads into anticipated difficulties, so be careful when considering an investment in one of these. You need to undertake some investigation to see if the market is right in being so pessimistic. It could be that it has over-reacted to temporary problems and the company will bounce back, giving you a large profit. The key is the quality of your investigation relative to others that have looked at it.

Understanding the tables in *The Financial Times*

Ever felt intimidated by all those columns of numbers in the *Financial Times* and other broadsheet newspapers? All those confusing fancy technical terms! Well, you are not the only one. But, just to prove how far you have come already – with your understanding of dividends, xd, dividend cover, dividend yield, etc. – I'll demonstrate that you can now understand those columns. Table 3.3 shows an extract from the *Financial Times*.

Note that the information provided in Monday's edition of the *FT* is different to that for the other days of the week, with dividend in pence, dividend cover, market capitalisation as well as the dates when the shares last went ex-dividend.

BAE Systems (making wings for Airbus plus defence equipment) has a dividend yield of 6.9%, greatly in excess of the return you get in a bank account. So for every pound you have to commit to buying BAE's shares you will receive an income of 6.9p (assuming that the dividend levels are maintained). This seems very attractive, but you need to bear in mind that the dividend amount may go down in future years – possibly to zero – and you may lose money if the share price declines. Higher risk goes with higher return.

Should you be disappointed if the dividend yield declines after buying? Well, that depends on what happens to the share price and the amount of dividends. Clearly if the yield falls because the dividend is cut and the share price falls because investors reckon the lower level will persist then you have reason to be disappointed.

However, if you buy a share for £5 when it paid a 35p dividend over the past year (a 7% dividend yield), and then over the following year

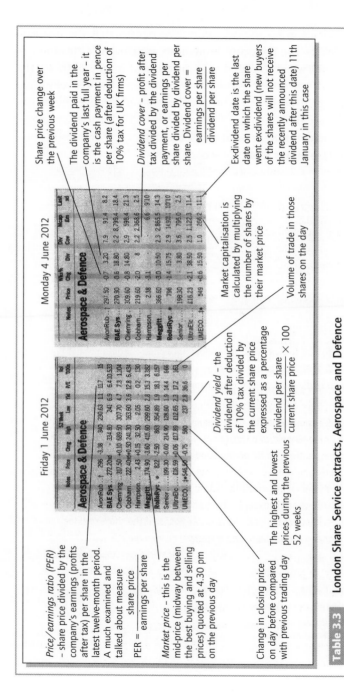

Price/earnings ratio (PER) – share price divided by the company's earnings (profits after tax) per share in the latest twelve-month period. A much examined and talked about measure

$$PER = \frac{\text{share price}}{\text{earnings per share}}$$

Market price – this is the mid-price (midway between the best buying and selling prices) quoted at 4.30 pm on the previous day

Change in closing price on day before compared with previous trading day

The highest and lowest prices during the previous 52 weeks

Dividend yield – the dividend after deduction of 10% tax divided by the current share price expressed as a percentage

$$\frac{\text{dividend per share}}{\text{current share price}} \times 100$$

Market capitalisation is calculated by multiplying the number of shares by their market price

Volume of trade in those shares on the day

Share price change over the previous week

The dividend paid in the company's last full year – it is the cash payment in pence per share (after deduction of 10% tax for UK firms)

Dividend cover – profit after tax divided by the dividend payment, or earnings per share divided by dividend per share. Dividend cover = earnings per share divided by dividend per share

Exdividend date is the last date on which the share went exdividend (new buyers of the shares will not receive the recently announced dividend after this date) 11th January in this case

Friday 1 June 2012

Monday 4 June 2012

Table 3.3 London Share Service extracts, Aerospace and Defence

Source: *The Financial Times*, 1 June and 4 June 2012

you see in the newspaper that the dividend yield falls to 3.5% you may want to take a closer look. If you find that the 35p dividend has been maintained and the company continues to be strong enough to carry on paying at this level and all that has happened is that the share price has doubled you have reason to be very pleased.

The relevant yield for you is the dividend amount divided by the price you paid for the share not the price at a later date. You locked in 7% because you paid £5 and not the new price of £10 (assuming the div is maintained at 35p). New investors will have to make do with a 3.5% yield but, given that share prices move every day and therefore the yield changes every day, they might be able to pick up the share at a higher yield if the price dips down for a while.

Most of the statistics are explained in the table but it might be worth adding a few points.

Price-earnings ratio

The *price to earnings ratio (PER or PE)* is an important measure used by most investors to get an idea of how high the share price is compared with the profit after tax per share reported in the past year. Many companies can be on high ratios, say a price of 30 times last year's earnings, if investors expect the earnings to grow rapidly over the next few years. A more normal ratio is around 7–15 times last year's earnings. A slow (no) growing firm might be on a PER less than 7. Those with no PER shown in the column made losses rather than profits in the last 12 months. There is a lot more on PER in Chapter 12.

Tax is deducted before you get the dividend

The dividend yields for UK firms shown in the *Financial Times* are calculated after deducting 10% tax from the *gross dividend*. The company sends you a cheque (the *net dividend*) but also pays the tax authorities 10% of the total gross dividend directly. You do not have to do anything about this except keep a record that tax was paid on your behalf. There is more on taxation for investors in Chapter 17. The dividends, on overseas companies are shown gross, i.e. without the tax deducted.

Capital gains (and losses)

While dividends are of great importance to most investors, we also need to take into account the bonus that comes from a rapidly appreciating share price. We saw in Chapter 1 how Rolls-Royce's shares had jumped from £1 to £8 in a decade. If your *investment horizon* (length of time you expect to hold) is this decade then you would have benefited more from the capital gain than from the dividends – although the dividends were pretty impressive too.

There are many companies that have such a wealth of projects expected to generate high returns (e.g. Google in its early days) that they sensibly save cash by not paying dividends for a decade or more so that they can finance investments. These should produce great profits in the years to come.

In these cases, for many years the only benefit you might receive is through the appreciation in the value of the shares. This is what happened to investors in Microsoft in the 1980s and 1990s. Despite dividends not being paid many investors, who had only put in a few thousand dollars, found themselves millionaires when they sold their holdings.

Share buy-backs and special dividends

An alternative way to return money to shareholders is for the company to repurchase issued shares. *Buy-backs* may also be a useful alternative when the company is unsure about the sustainability of a possible increase in the normal cash dividend. A stable policy may be pursued on dividends, then, as and when surplus cash arises, shares are repurchased. This two-track approach avoids sending an over-optimistic signal about future growth through underlying dividend levels.

A second possible approach to returning funds without signalling that all future dividends will be raised abnormally is to pay a *special dividend*. This is the same as a normal dividend but usually bigger and paid on a one-off basis.

Share repurchases are permitted under UK law, subject to the requirement that the firm gain the permission of shareholders. The rules of the London Stock Exchange must also be obeyed. These are generally aimed at avoiding the creation of an artificial market in the company's shares.

Perks

Fancy a cheap trip or a discount off a dress, a house, or a car? A few companies offer their shareholders freebies. These might be substantial discounts off their goods and services or merely a £20 goody bag handed out at the AGM. These perks help promote the sale of the company products, e.g. Persimmon might entice the sale of a house with a 2% discount, and the shareholder gains a little extra, engendering greater loyalty. Table 3.4 gives some examples of shareholder perks.

Some of the minimum shareholding levels are quite high so you need to weigh up the extent to which you might benefit from the perk against the lost opportunity of investing that money elsewhere. If you would have bought into the company on its investment merits anyway then all well and good. But buying because of the perk may confuse your investment judgement, so make sure the perk is of sufficient value to you – don't let the tail wag the dog. Also, you may find that you can get more discount negotiating on your own, especially with hotels.

Watch out for minimum holding periods before you qualify for the perk – this could be a year or more. Also, keep track of the company policy on perks; they can change or disappear from one year to the next.

Table 3.4 **Some examples of shareholder perks**

Aga Rangemaster Group plc	Holders of 5,000+ shares are entitled to a 10% discount on purchases totalling £500 or more, including Aga, Divertimenti and Fired Earth. Shares held for a minimum of 90 days.
Associated British Foods plc	Shareholders who attend the AGM will receive a free gift, typically consisting of samples of the company's products, each with a retail value of about £30.
Bellway plc	Eligible shareholders wishing to purchase a new Bellway home are entitled to a discount of £2,000 per £25,000 or pro rata on part thereof, off the purchase price.
Bloomsbury Publishing plc	35% off the recommended retail price of all Bloomsbury books.
Brown (N) Group plc	20% discount on purchases from the group's mail order catalogues.
Fuller, Smith & Turner plc	Shareholder Discount Card which offers a 50% reduction on Fuller, Smith & Turner hotel prices (Fri–Sat; 10% Sun–Thur; subject to availability). The Discount Card is issued bi-annually. Minimum of 250 shares.
Greene King plc	Shareholder vouchers are issued once a year to holders on the register at the end of July each year. The vouchers offer discounts on food and drink at Greene King pubs, Loch Fyne restaurants and local pubs. Minimum 100 shares.
Groupe Eurotunnel SA	Eligible shareholders are entitled to a 30% discount on standard Eurotunnel tickets for three return journeys or six one-way journeys per calendar year. Minimum of 750 shares.
Inchcape plc	15% discount on service, parts and accessories. £100 off the retail price of used cars. £100 off the retail price of new cars. Minimum 100 shares.
Marks & Spencer Group plc	Shareholders are sent vouchers each year, offering discounts across M&S product ranges.
Moss Bros Group plc	20% discount on full price merchandise at the company's retail outlets.
Mothercare plc	Shareholders owning 500 or more shares are entitled to a 10% discount on up to £500 of merchandise.
Persimmon plc	2% discount on the price of a new property, subject to a maximum discount of £4,000 in any 12 month period. 1,000 shares (held for at least 12 months).

Source: Hargreaves Lansdown http://www.hl.co.uk/shares/shareholder-perks/shareholder-perks

4

What do stockbrokers do?

With an evening coat and a white tie, anybody, even a stockbroker, can gain a reputation for being civilized.

Oscar Wilde

Stockbrokers perform a very simple role – they help investors to carry out a trade. It would be very intimidating and time-consuming if, when you wanted to buy or sell some shares, you had to traipse along to a stock exchange to find another investor willing to transact with you. Even with telephones and internet technology there are good reasons for not encouraging a large volume of investor-to-investor dealing – it is difficult to get all the legal and technical elements right. To avoid inexperienced and ill-equipped traders gumming up the smooth running of the markets the London Stock Exchange insists that its trades are generally conducted through a few registered and regulated stockbrokers.

This does not mean that you cannot buy or sell with another investor directly *off-exchange* – there are simple forms to allow you to do this – but when there is difficulty in locating strangers willing to do a deal then it is better to use professional intermediaries to expedite matters.

They are not that posh anymore

There is a rather old-fashioned image of a stockbroker wearing pin-stripes, bowler hat and talking with an authoritative upper-class twang. Long lunches at the club to discuss your investments are long gone. Hardly anyone wears the pin-stripe suit and most don't even wear ties these days. They are just ordinary people (with ordinary accents) trying to provide a quality service.

So, do not be intimidated at the thought of having to initiate a conversation with these men and women. They will efficiently set you up with an account; help guide you through the technicalities of trading, and work hard to get you the shares you want at the right price. They are on your side. Stock-broking is a very competitive business and they are very keen on making things easy for you so that you stick around and ask them to undertake more transactions through them. Regard yourself as being in charge and shop around.

Types of broker

There are two types of broker:

- *Private-client*, also called *retail brokers*, act for investors.
- *Corporate brokers* act on behalf of companies. When a company is thinking about issuing more shares it might contact its broker for advice on market conditions and an estimate of the likely price that it can get away with. The broker liaises with the stock exchange and investors. The broker will represent (public relations stuff) the company to the market, providing information and analysis on the firm for investors.

Given that this book is for investors, we will concentrate here on private-client brokers.

Setting things up with a broker

Before being able to deal you will have to *register* with a private-client broker – this simply involves providing a few details about yourself. The broker will check your creditworthiness (e.g. banker's reference). Anti-money-laundering requirements mean that you have to prove you are who you say you are. The whole checking process may take two weeks or so. Many brokers then set up an account so that you can deposit money into it. This will reassure the broker that you will have money to pay for a trade in a timely fashion.

There are three main types of service provided by retail brokers:

1 execution-only,

2 advisory,

3 discretionary.

Which of these is most suitable for you depends on your circumstances.

Execution-only (or dealing-only) service

Here the broker carries out your purchase or sale order as instructed without offering any investment advice. It is the cheapest way to buy and sell shares. A typical minimum *commission* is around £10–20, but it can be as little as £6. (You need to be trading 100 times each quarter to qualify for the £6 service).

These figures would apply if you were buying, say, £1,000 of shares. Charges normally rise as the size of order increases. So for a £5,000 bargain £20–30 is more typical. However, brokers have become so keen to gain business that it is possible to deal for £8–10 or so, even for orders of £25,000.

The figures given so far are for online dealing. If you use phone and postal dealing then the typical ranges of fees are somewhat higher: minimum commission of around £15–25; for £5,000 bargains, £25–80; for £25,000 bargains, £50–200.

Some brokers charge even when you are not dealing, through monthly or quarterly account fees, which can be as much as £10 per month. The justification is that the fee covers the cost of distributing dividends and issuing statements.

Shop around! There are over 50 dealing-only brokers in the UK to choose from. This type of service is very popular, with over 90% of investors now in the habit of using an execution-only broker.

Execution is not for everyone

Execution-only dealing is particularly appropriate if you have the time and inclination to make investment decisions on your own. If you have greater confidence in your own research and judgement than in the broker's, then execution-only is the service for you. The downside is that you will not be able to discuss your ideas with a broker. It is also said that you will miss out on hot tips – but then, selecting on the basis of hot tips is not investing but speculating, and is generally unprofitable.

Advisory dealing service

Under this arrangement the broker will give you investment advice, but the decision on whether to buy or sell rests with you. The broker will not take any investment decisions without your authority.

Roughly one-quarter of UK investors have opened these 'dealing with advice' accounts. This is the more traditional stock-broking service in which the broker knows the client sufficiently well for meaningful discussion of ideas and strategies. It allows the investor to test ideas with someone who is in touch with the market full-time. Also, broker reports on companies or sectors, newsletters or market reviews may be sent to clients as well as tax advice and portfolio valuation.

Advice costs

The advisory service costs more than execution-only. The broker earns money through charging commission on each deal rather than by charging for advice directly. A typical minimum trans-action charge would be between £20 and £50. This rises to £40–100 for £5,000 deals and £200–300 for £25,000 transactions. The cost varies tremendously from broker to broker, as does the quality of the service.

Who initiates?

Some advisory brokers go further for their clients than others. While many will wait for a call from an investor before offering advice, others are more willing to initiate the contact.

Taking the initiative one stage further, some brokers now differentiate between their advisory dealing service and their advisory portfolio management service. The *advisory dealing service* is taken to be a reactive one in which the broker gives advice after being asked for it, whereas under the *advisory portfolio management service* the client is contacted once or twice per month with advice on their portfolio – this is usually when there is a good reason, such as news on a particular stock, sectors, etc.

Churn

With the advisory portfolio management approach the broker is knowledgeable about the client's overall financial profile and can advise appropriately. One drawback with this type of arrangement is that the investor might be encouraged to deal frequently – good for brokers but, more often than not, very bad for the wealth of investors.

You can ask some brokers to accept a fee based on the size of the investment fund they handle for you, that is, an asset-based fee system. This removes some of the incentive for the stockbroker to *churn* your portfolio (make unnecessary trades to generate fees – nowadays churn is less of a concern given the pressure applied by the regulator, the Financial Conduct Authority, to ensure that stockbrokers' compliance officers are monitoring accounts to prevent churn – they ask their managers to justify the level of trading on an account). It also gives an incentive to increase the size of the pot. Thus the broker may choose to go into cash rather than sticking with shares at times of market exuberance, so that total asset size is preserved.

Discretionary service

Under this type of service the broker is paid to manage the investor's portfolio at the broker's discretion. Thus the broker takes decisions on which shares to buy and sell without consulting the investor on each deal. The client is informed after the event.

Giving the broker authorisation to act before getting the investor's approval allows the snatching of good opportunities as they arise in fast-moving markets. One of the common complaints from advisory brokers is that their clients are not always near a telephone – oddly enough, they like to live a life beyond their portfolio – and so fleeting chances are missed as permission to buy is not given quickly.

Furthermore, many clients simply do not want to spend time managing their portfolios. They don't want to devote effort to developing investment skills. They therefore place their money in the hands of professionals. Prior to running your portfolio the broker will meet you to gain an understanding of your particular circumstances, your investment aims and any restrictions you would like to place on the portfolio (e.g. no investment in tobacco or arms).

Only around 5% of UK investors have discretionary portfolio management accounts with brokers. One of the reasons for the low take-up is that brokers generally insist on a minimum portfolio size of £50,000 (although a few go as low as £25,000). Some set the minimum at £100,000 or even higher. The average discretionary portfolio is around a quarter of a million.

Another reason is the cost of the service. Not only are investors usually charged commission (at about the same level as advisory clients) on each transaction but they are also charged an *annual fee* related to the total value of the portfolio. This is generally between 0.5 and 1%. Some brokers have high dealing charges and low annual fees, whereas others charge a mere £20 or so for each transaction but load the costs on to the annual fee while a few now offer a fee-only service for most discretionary clients. The amount you pay depends on the frequency of trading – the discretion over which you have granted to the broker. This means that you must be on your guard against churning. It is disturbing that very few brokers offer to charge on the basis of the returns they achieve.

Choosing a stockbroker

There are many ways of finding a stockbroker. The London Stock Exchange (*www.londonstockexchange.com*) publishes a complete list of its members. The Association of Private Client Investment Managers and Stockbrokers (APCIMS) provides lots of information on their website *www.apcims.co.uk* (or telephone 020 7448 7100), including stockbrokers' contact names, addresses, telephone numbers and an outline of the kinds of services offered. Of course, you can find many stockbrokers listed in the Yellow Pages.

Investors are regularly surveyed for their opinions on broker performance and costs in investment magazines such as *Investors Chronicle*. Investors also find brokers through personal recommendation.

Choosing a broker means selecting the right combination of cost and services. The following selection criteria may help you draw up a shortlist of brokers and make a final selection.

Charges

Of course, the lower the commissions for trading the better, but you should allow for the possibility of improved service at extra cost. An important aspect of improved service is the effort put into *price improvement* which is when the broker takes action to obtain better prices than those shown on brokers' stock exchange screens. They might do this by haggling with a market maker (these traders help to set the price of shares – described in Chapter 5).

The charging structure will make a big difference to your choice of broker. For example, an investor who does not want to pay for advice and trades many times each month with bargain sizes of around £5,000 will prefer a broker who charges a low fixed rate regardless of bargain size, say £20 each time. Another trader, who buys and sells £1,000 of shares, may prefer a broker who charges a percentage of the amount of the trade, say, 1.5%.

If you are a *buy-and-hold* investor, with few transactions, commission costs will not be a great concern. But if you are very active the charges mount up dramatically. Then you may opt for the cheapest mode of transacting – usually online, though some telephone brokers can also be very cheap.

Location

The possibility of being able to talk to a broker face-to-face may lead investors to favour a local broker. This can be particularly valuable for discretionary and advisory portfolio management, where the broker needs to know the investor's circumstances and investing objectives. Local brokers may also be knowledgeable about companies in the region.

Contact

In surveys, investors usually place the ability to contact brokers at the top of their worry list.

- There are many complaints about telephone lines being busy when a client wishes to deal. People can be put on hold for 20 minutes or more. This can seem like an eternity when you are trying to sell and the market is falling like a stone.
- Brokers are also criticised for not calling back when they promised to do so.
- Online orders are often executed very slowly at busy times, as the IT systems suffer from overload.

Unfortunately, quality of contact is one of those factors that you do not really find out about until you experience it. However, it might be worth asking other clients of your shortlisted brokers if they have any complaints. It could be useful to be able to switch to telephone dealing if the online system is down, and vice versa. So consider a broker that gives you this flexibility.

Administration

The second factor most complained about is the quality of the administration. Record keeping is sometimes poor, as is the administration of dividends and taxation matters. Often the paperwork reaches the investor weeks after the event.

You do not have to put up with this: other brokers are highly praised for the speed and efficiency of their administration.

Expertise

You need a broker who is well resourced, has access to high-quality external data and attracts talented managers. This is especially important if you are asking for portfolio management services. You do not want your nest egg managed by a graduate trainee trying to learn on the job. Ask what experience the firm has in managing portfolios of the type and size you have in mind.

Performance

Unfortunately independently constructed league tables of portfolio managers' performance are not available and so comparison is all but impossible. Brokers do provide statistics, but you must view them with caution.* Recommendation may be your main hope.

Interest

Brokers hold money in cash accounts on behalf of investors. Some of these accounts offer miserly rates of interest of under 1%. If you are likely to deposit substantial sums with a broker you need to ask what rate of interest you will receive prior to the purchase of shares. Also, if you need temporary credit, what limit will the broker allow you to go up to?

---

* There is a problem in compiling and comparing statistics on performance because the data brokers provide is specific to the particular needs of the clients. For example, is the client risk averse on how diverse is their general portfolio, i.e. how much investment do they have outside of shares?

Why stick at one broker?

About half of UK investors open accounts with more than one broker – it does not cost anything to open two or three accounts. One reason for multiple accounts is to avoid the frustration of not being able to contact a broker – if one is not picking up the phone another might. Investors may also require specific services that their main broker either does not provide or supplies at a higher price. Also, you can compare quality of service and cost and push more of your business the way of the better broker.

Instructions and instructions

You may be thinking that you simply phone up the broker (or use the online service) and say 'buy' or 'sell'. Think again. There are many different types of orders you can make.

At best

'At best'† means that the trade is completed immediately at the best price available. Prior to you saying to your broker that you would like to buy (or sell) you would have asked for the broker to tell you the current prices in the market – the prices other traders are offering to buy or sell. If you like the price then you can instruct the broker to do a deal.

But there is a problem. In the few seconds between you saying you would like to buy and the broker actually entering the market with an order the price may change. Thus the broker is unable to obtain the shares at the price he or she quoted to you. It might not suit you or the broker to just walk away, and keep coming back until the price stops moving. So to make sure you complete a transaction you leave an 'at best' order where you accept whatever the market is offering at the time of the deal.

---

† Also called a *market order*.

Limit order

If the uncertainty of dealing at best is too much, you can place a *limit order*. Here you specify the maximum price at which you are willing to buy or the minimum price at which you are willing to sell.

The order can stay on the system until it is fulfilled (up to 90 days) or until cancelled (*good-till-cancelled* order) or until a fixed expiry date is reached. An online limit order is usually only *good for the day* (you have to re-enter it for the next day).

Fill or kill

Whoever came up with these names watched one too many action thrillers! With a fill or kill order a maximum (minimum) price is stated. If the deal cannot be executed in its entirety at this price or better, the entire order expires. This is also called an *all or none* order.

Execute and eliminate

Now we are really sounding like we are hiring assassins! An execute and eliminate order means that the transaction is completed in part or in full immediately. A price limit is set by the investor. If not completed immediately the order expires on the spot. If only some of an order is fulfilled the remainder expires. The broker buys or sells what he or she can and 'eliminates' the shortfall.

Stop-loss order

This is a order that you can leave with a broker once you own the shares. The broker is instructed to sell if the shares fall below a stated price. The idea is to protect your portfolio against a dramatic and sudden downward move, thus protecting the bulk of your funds.

Personally, I do not see the point in them. If you are 'investing' rather than 'speculating on market moves' then you will have thoroughly analysed the company and judged it a good one to hold at that price. If it falls then it is an even better buy! If the fundamental strengths of the company have deteriorated then this may induce a sell, but not a fall in share price *per se*.

Ways of paying for your shares

- Send a cheque in the post. Your broker may not be willing to buy for you until the cheque is cleared.
- Visit a high street broker and pay there and then, for example by credit card.
- Pay by debit card over the telephone.
- Open a deposit account with the broker or bank. Your broker is able to draw money from the account on your behalf at any time to settle deals.

Internet dealing

The majority of execution-only share trades are conducted online. Internet dealing has many advantages: it can be very cheap and quick to deal; and you can trade wherever you like, without having to communicate with a broker in normal office hours.

Furthermore, your PC/tablet/mobile can be used to download vast amounts of information, including real-time price quotes, market news and commentary, charts of share prices and volume of trades, detailed company information, brokers' reports and forecasts – see Chapter 7.

In a typical Internet-based transaction, when you have viewed the prices on screen and placed an order you are given 15 seconds to accept or reject the deal. If you click 'accept' the transaction is completed immediately and a *contract note* (telling you the price paid, etc.) is emailed.

While online trading is low cost, there are still some problems:

- Some systems are crash-prone. Computer failure can be very frustrating, so always have a back-up method of trading. It might be worth opening accounts at two or more brokers.

▓ If you are thinking of buying a computer principally in order to trade, then the setup costs need to be considered.

▓ The security of information in cyberspace is a worry for many people, although encryption technology is helping the situation.

▓ Internet dealing usually requires the use of a nominee account to allow for speedy and cheap settlement. This means that, even though you are the beneficial holder of the shares, the company simply sees the broker's nominee name as the holder, meaning that you may have difficulty receiving information from the company. There is more on nominee holdings of shares in Chapter 5.

▓ The simplicity and speed of trading may lead investors to trade too frequently or to make reckless trades – many day traders lose a fortune in transaction costs.

▓ Watch out for silly mistakes resulting in purchase of the wrong number of shares by punching on the wrong key.

Transferring shares without brokers

It is possible to complete an *off-market transfer* without the use of a broker if the transfer is between people you know, such as friends or spouses. You need to complete a *stock transfer form*, which is available free from the company registrar, or from brokers, banks or on the Internet‡ (legal stationers will charge you for the form). The transfer form on the back of share certificates is for use when you are trading in the stock market, so is not suitable for DIY share selling or gifting. You need to have a share certificate to complete a transaction without a broker. If the shares are held in a broker's nominee account (see Chapter 5) the broker will charge for the transfer.

Stamp duty does not apply to transfers between spouses or gift transfers. For other transfers the completed form is sent to Her

---

‡ Make sure you download the UK version.

Majesty's Revenue and Customs with a cheque for stamp duty of 0.5%. The stamp office will return the form (after stamping it) for you to send to the registrar of the company who will issue a new certificate.

chapter

5

What happens once you have decided to trade?

There is tide in the affairs of men which, taken at the flood, leads on to
fortune; omitted, all the voyage of life is bound in shallows and in
miseries.

J. Caesar, W. Shakespeare

You have now reached the exciting stage: after setting up an
account with a broker and figuring out which shares you want
to buy, you can now actually go into the market place to obtain
them.

When you've contacted your broker they will give you not one
price, but two. The first is the price at which you can sell the
shares, the other is the price at which you can buy. To understand
what is going on we need to step back and learn about the mechanisms at play in the stock market and how the broker interacts
with them.

Older ways of trading

Traditionally, shares were traded between two traders, face to
face. A few stock exchanges around the world still have a place
where buyers and sellers or their representatives meet to trade.
For example, the New York Stock Exchange (NYSE) continues

to make some use of a large trading floor with thousands of face-to-face deals taking place every working day (*open outcry trading*).

This is the traditional image of a stock market, and if television reporters have a story about what is going on in the world's security markets, they often show an image of traders rushing around, talking quickly amid a flurry of small slips of paper on the NYSE trading floor. To an outsider it seems amazing that anyone can hear or understand what is happening, let alone trade shares, but the people who work on floors like this revel in the bustling atmosphere.

The move to silence

Most trading now, however, is done silently in front of banks of computers, with deals being completed in nano-seconds. The stress levels for those dealing remain as high, if not higher, than ever, as now a slight mistake with a finger on a keyboard can cause mayhem.

Quote-driven trading

Quote-driven trading is how most stock exchanges used to be operated – and many still are. With this type of approach, *market makers* (*dealers*) give a price at which they would buy (lower price) or sell (higher price), and make their profits on the margin between buying and selling. The market maker's *bid* is the price at which they are willing to buy and *offer* (or *ask*) is the price at which they are willing to sell.

What happens in computerised trading? When you mention the company name, the broker immediately enters in its company code. In the UK, the computer is linked to the London Stock Exchange (LSE) Automated Quotations (SEAQ™, pronounced 'see-ack') system. This is a system for distributing the prices offered by market makers. Within milliseconds of you mentioning your interest in the company the broker has access to all the prices that different market makers are willing to pay as well as all the prices they are willing to sell the shares for.* (Note that not all UK shares are traded through SEAQ. Most are traded through other LSE systems and so where the broker's computer screen goes to fetch prices depends on where in the LSE's systems the shares are traded – we look at them later.)

Criticism of trading systems based on market makers quoting bid and offer prices has focused on the size of the middleman's (the market maker's) margin. Many investors wondered why it was necessary to have market makers at all rather than buyers and sellers agreeing a single price. After all, the difference between the bid and offer price can be 20% or more. This idea led to the development of order-driven trading.

Order-driven trading

Order-driven trading is where buyers (via brokers) trade with sellers at a single price so that there is no bid–offer spread. Prices from those willing to buy or sell are displayed electronically and buyers and sellers are matched electronically. The big advantage with this system is that prices are transparent and available to everyone with access to this type of information. The disadvantage is that there is no guarantee that buy and sell orders can be matched, whereas trading through a market maker guarantees execution of the deal.†

Most stock exchanges in the world now operate order-driven systems (sometimes called *matched-bargain systems* or *order book trading*). The LSE has *SETS* (*Stock Exchange Electronic Trading System*), and I will use this as an example to explain how order-driven trading works.

---

* If you are dealing online instead of speaking to a broker, you will call up the broker's website using your user ID and password. You will then input the name of the company or its code and view the prices.

† Up to a certain quantity of shares.

SETS

SETS is the electronic order book for liquid shares (shares in large companies which are traded frequently) on the Main Market of the LSE as well as some shares on the more lightly regulated exchange run by LSE, called the Alternative Investment Market (AIM) .

It executes millions of trades per day in milliseconds. Traders, via brokers, enter the prices at which they are willing to buy or sell as well as the quantity of shares they want to trade. They can then wait for the market to move to the price they set as their limit. Alternatively, they can instruct brokers to transact immediately at the best price currently available on the order book system.

Trades are then executed by the system if there is a match between a buy order price and a sell order price. These prices are displayed anonymously to the entire market.

An example of prices and quantities is shown Figure 5.1 – a reproduction of a SETS screen as seen by brokers. This particular example is for GlaxoSmithKline, stock symbol GSK, and the type of share is Ordinary with a nominal issued value of 25p.

On the left-hand side of the screen is the order book, the list of buy orders, shown on the left, and sell orders, shown on the right. So, we can observe for the company GSK's shares that someone (or more than one person) has entered that they are willing to buy 300 shares at a maximum price of 1732p (bottom line in Figure 5.1). Someone else has entered that they would like to sell 686 shares at a minimum price of 1764p.

Clearly the computer cannot match these two orders and neither of these two investors will be able to trade. They will either have to adjust their limit prices or wait until the market moves in their favour.

As we travel up the screen there is a closing of the gap between the prices buyers are willing to pay and the offering price of sellers and the buy and sell prices come closer to a match. The yellow strip displays the closest available matching prices. There is one

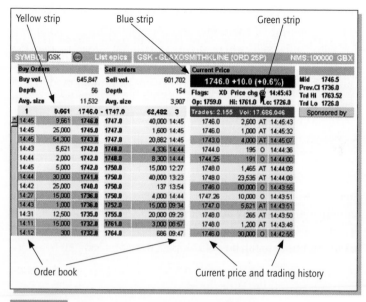

Figure 5.1   SETS screen, London Stock Exchange

Source: www.advfn.com

buy order for 9,661 shares at 1746p, and there are three sell orders totalling 62,482 shares at 1747p.

Above the yellow strip are the totals for buy and sell orders. There are 56 buy orders for a total of 645,847 shares, and 154 sell orders for a total of 601,702 shares. As you can see, the screen only displays a small number of these buy and sell orders, those closest to the last executed prices. Those using the screen can scroll down to see further buy and sell orders.

On the right-hand side is the current price and trading history. The current price for GSK is 1746p, the last AT (automatic trade generated by the SETS computer when there is a match) trade to be executed. The blue strip denotes that the price has increased, by 10p, 0.6 per cent, over the previous day's closing price of 1736p. If a price decreases since the start of the day the strip will be red.

The green strip displays the number of trades carried out so far on this day (2,155) and the volume of shares traded (17,686,046.).

Below is the trading history, detailing the share price, the volume traded, the time of the trade, and the type of trade – AT stands for automatic trade where the SETS computer system matches orders automatically, and O stands for an ordinary trade carried out by market makers (yes, market makers are now allowed to post their prices on the SETS system). The last trade was carried out at 14.45.43 (about a quarter to three) for 2,600 shares at 1746p.

These screens are available to market participants (mostly brokers) at all times and so they are able to judge where to pitch their price limits. For example, if I was a buyer of 5,000 shares entering the market I would not be inclined to offer more than 1747p given the current state of supply and demand. On the other hand, if I was a seller of 9,000 shares I would recognise that the price offered would not have to fall below 1746p to attract buyers.

If, however, I was a buyer of 70,000 shares rather than just 5,000 I have two options: I could set a maximum price of 1747p in which case I would transact for 62,482 immediately but would leave the other 7,518 unfilled order in the market hoping for a general market price decline; alternatively, I could set my limit at 1748p, in which case I could transact with those investors prepared to sell at 1747p and 1748p. The unfilled orders of the sellers at 1748p (4,336 + 8,300 − 7,518 = 5,118) are carried forward on SETS.

So which system is best?

Supporters of the older quote-driven system say that a major problem with the order-driven system is that there may be few or no shares offered at prices close to a market clearing rate and so little trade can take place. In other words, the market can be very illiquid. There may indeed be times when no sellers are posting sensible prices and other times when buyers are scarce. This is when the quote-driven system may be more liquid because market makers who make a book in a company's shares must continuously offer prices and are obliged to trade at the price shown.

By way of counter-criticism, it is alleged there have been times when it has been difficult to contact market makers to trade at their displayed prices, even though in theory they are obliged to make themselves available to quote and trade at bid and offer prices throughout the trading day. Ideally, we need the benefits of both systems; and that is what we are moving towards.

To improve trading liquidity on SETS, in 2007 the system was modified so that market makers can now post prices on it. Thus it offers a continuous order book with automatic execution, but also has market makers providing continuous bid and offer prices for many shares. It is thought that by having the two systems combined there will be tighter bid–offer spreads, greater transparency of trades and improved liquidity.

Clearing

When your trade has been completed and reported to the exchange it is necessary to *clear* it; the exchange must ensure that all reports of the trade are reconciled so that the buyer and the seller are in agreement as to the number and the price of shares traded. The exchange also checks that the buyer and seller have the cash and securities to do the deal. Also, the company registrar, which keeps a record of who owns the shares, is notified of the change in ownership.

These days, clearing frequently does not just mean checking that a buyer and a seller agree on the deal; the clearing house also is a *central counterparty*, acting as a buyer to every seller and as a seller to every buyer. This eliminates the risk of failure to complete a deal by guaranteeing that shares will be delivered against payment and vice versa. So, technically you are transacting with an ultra-safe organisation which is very unlikely to renege on the deal. For most of its UK share trading the LSE uses LCH.Clearnet as its clearer.

Settlement

After clearing the transfer of ownership from seller to buyer has to take place; this is called *settlement*. For the LSE, as in most of Europe, share settlement is T+3. It simply means that shares are transferred to new owners three days after the trade takes place.

Before 1996 the transfer of shares involved a tedious paperchase between investors, brokers, company registrars, market makers and the Exchange. The new system, called CREST, provides an electronic means of settlement and registration. This 'paperless' system is cheaper and quicker – ownership is transferred with a few strokes of a keyboard (referred to as *dematerialisation*).

Under the CREST system, shares are often held in the name of a *nominee company* rather than in the name of the *beneficial owner*, that is, you, the new owner. Brokers and investment managers run these nominee accounts. So your broker would hold your shares electronically in a nominee account and would arrange settlement through membership of the CREST system. There might be dozens of investors with shares held by a particular nominee company. The nominee company appears as the *registered owner* of the shares as far as the company (say, BA or BT) is concerned. Despite this, you will receive all dividends and the proceeds from the sale of the shares.

Placing shares in a nominee account can remove a lot of administrative work for investors. If you wish to sell shares you hold in certificated form, it is necessary to sign a stock transfer form and send it with the share certificate to your broker, who will then check the form and pass it on to the company registrar.

Postal dealing and settlement is clearly impossible within the T+3 settlement time, as well as being more fiddly for brokers. Many brokers allow you to delay settling a deal beyond three days (say T+5, T+10, T+20). This is subject to special arrangement, and more costs. So those clients who use the nominee system will be settled at T+3 while for private investors who prefer to receive certificates, settlement is more likely to be T+10.

Opposing the CREST wave

Many investors oppose the advance of CREST nominee accounts because under such a system they do not automatically receive annual reports and other documentation, such as an invitation to the company's annual general meeting.‡ You could also lose the potential to vote – after all, the company does not know who the beneficial owners are. (However some brokers will vote at shareholder meetings as per your instructions.) Shareholders can also miss out on perks.

Those investors who take their ownership of a part of a company seriously can insist on remaining outside CREST. In this way they receive share certificates and are treated as the real owners of the business. This is more expensive when share dealing, but that is not a great concern for investors who trade infrequently. Another advantage of being outside the nominee system is that you are not tied to a single broker for all your deals. Around half of UK shareholders still hold their shares in certificated form.

A compromise

Personal membership of CREST (sponsored membership) allows you to be both the legal owner via CREST and the beneficial owner of the shares, and also benefit from rapid (and cheap) electronic share settlement.§ The owner will be sent all company communications and retain voting rights.

However, this can be more expensive than the nominee CREST accounts run by brokers. Personal CREST account costs vary from broker to broker. Some do not charge, while others ask for up to £100 per year. Some brokers make an extra charge for each trade through a personal CREST account (for example, Charles Stanley asks for an additional £10).

If you are thinking of opting for a nominee service you might like to ask the following:

■ What charges will be levied for what services?

---

‡ With the standard nominee service offered by brokers, investors can request that reports and accounts, perks and invitations to company meetings be passed on. They may be charged extra for this.
§ The broker still acts as sponsor, even though the accounts are held in the shareholder's name.

- How will the investments be protected while in the nominee account?
- Will I receive annual reports and accounts, the right to vote, invitations to AGMs and extraordinary general meetings, and perks?

Alternatives to SETS

Trading on SETS is for companies whose trading is liquid so there are plenty of shares traded each day, as was apparent in Figure 5.1 where over seven million shares of GSK were traded on one day. There are other means of trading for less frequently traded shares.

SETSqx

SETSqx (*Stock Exchange Electronic Trading Service – quotes and crosses*) trades in Main Market and LSE's AIM shares which are less liquid and not traded on SETS.

SETSqx combines order book technology with quote-driven trading and periodic auctions. It works like this: A single market maker's quote can be displayed if a market maker is interested in quoting a price. (Ideally, the exchange would like many market makers' quoting prices so that competition encourages keener prices for share owners.)

An investor wanting to trade with a market maker can do so in the normal way, but can also connect, usually via brokers, to the electronic system and put onto the system's screen an order for shares stating a price at which they would like to trade, either to sell or to buy – particularly useful if there are no market makers in that share. If someone else on the system likes the displayed price they can phone the originator and a deal is done.

This may still leave some orders for trades unexecuted (i.e. no one phones up and trades at the advertised price). To cope with this, or to trade shares anonymously, throughout the day there are four auctions, at 8am, 11am, 3pm and 4.35pm (end of day) in which investors make bids and the system matches up buyers and sellers and generates prices calculated from all matched bids and offers during the auction period. All Main Market shares trade on either SETS or SETSqx.

SEAQ

The third system used by LSE (for 700 small companies on AIM), called SEAQ, is purely market maker based. They quote prices that your broker can see on his/her computer.

The market makers' prices are quoted as *firm* prices. That is, the LSE insists that the market maker trade at these prices if a broker (investor) has been attracted to do a deal based on the posted prices. They cannot change them when they are contacted by the broker if the transaction is below *the normal market size* (*NMS*). (This is set at approximately 2.5% of the average daily share turnover.)

For deals larger than the NMS, the market maker is allowed to change prices and will give the broker a price when he/she calls. Of course prices can be changed at any time on the SEAQ system so the market maker can adjust in response to the weight of buying and selling pressure, and in response to what other market makers are offering.

When your broker buys or sells for you the trade is reported to the central computer and disseminated to market participants (usually within three minutes). This means that everyone is aware of the price at which recent trades were completed.

After the deal

The next day you should receive a *contract note* in the post (or by email). This will state the price, the time of the deal, the number of shares, the broker's commission and the charge of 0.5% of the value of your purchase in *stamp duty* (this is a form of taxation that applies to purchase only).

Check the details to make sure they match your expectations and file the note so you have a record (it will be useful when it comes to filling out tax returns). If you have a broking account linked to your bank account, then the broker will debit (credit) the account three business days after the transaction. If you have opted to receive *share certificates* then these will be sent to you by the registrar of the firm in which you now hold shares.

The advanced stuff – direct market access

Once you are a little more familiar with trading you can pay for a special service called *direct market access* (*DMA*), allowing you to trade directly in the stock market, placing buy and sell orders into the LSEs electronic order book (e.g. SETS) alongside the professionals. To do this you need to download the necessary software from a DMA provider – a service offered by some stockbrokers. Despite the direct link into the market you will still be trading via a broker when using DMA.

To use DMA you will subscribe for a 'Level 2 package' (see page 108) so that you can see the buy and sell orders placed by other investors, and then be able to watch your order flash up on the SETS or SETSqx screen.

There are several advantages in inputting your own buy and sell prices:

- **Better prices and a greater chance of execution**. Say you want to sell shares in a company and observe a quoted spread of 200–202p. A non-DMA trader could expect to get 200p, but a DMA trader might place a limit order of say 201.5p to entice a deal. Being able to see everyone else's buy and sell orders including the amounts on offer allows you to get a feel of the balance of supply and demand, which helps in selecting where to pitch your price.

- **Speed**. Your order goes into the system in a fraction of a second after you press your keyboard button and may be completed immediately. Also you can trade on breaking news. For example, other traders may have left sell orders on the SETS system. When positive news is announced for a company (e.g. a big contract win) these other investors may be slow in changing their prices. If you have DMA and spot the news early enough you might bag a bargain.

▪ **Testing and adjusting prices**. You will be able to see where your order lies on the LSE's order book and how close you are to getting it filled. This allows you to adjust the price if you wish to find a counterparty and trade immediately.

The cost of a DMA service varies tremendously. Furthermore, the sector is evolving as brokers supplying the software and access arrangements compete vigorously with each other. For infrequent traders, the software and Level 2 data can cost hundreds of pounds per year, but if you trade, say, 15 times or more in a month these costs might be waived. Much depends on the special offers available at brokers. DMA is really only suitable for frequent traders (at least five times per week) who have the time to watch markets for hours on end. Not everyone is able to obtain DMA because brokers vet clients to ensure they have sufficient knowledge to trade in this way.

6

What do stock markets do?

One of the very nice things about investing in the stock market is that you learn about all different aspects of the economy. It's your window into a very large world.

Ron Chernow

Stock markets are not casinos, despite them often being portrayed as such. Many participants in the stock markets are looking for short-term speculative gains, but most are genuine long-term investors. Stock markets facilitate the raising of money by companies, not least by providing a market place for sales of shares between investors.

The recent growth of exchanges in China illustrates the reasons why such markets are so important. Here is a communist government placing a very high priority on the raising of private capital.

- What are the compelling attractions of these markets?
- What do stock markets provide that you need?
- Why are they an essential centre piece of a modern market economy?

This chapter helps to answer these questions.

A worldwide phenomenon

Over the past 100 years, stock markets have prospered. The old ones have grown in size, and dozens of new ones have sprung up all over the globe – now over 140 countries have stock exchanges. One measure of their size is to look at the market value of the shares traded on them. This is the *market capitalisation* of the companies, which means the price of each share multiplied by the total number of shares the company has issued to investors. According to figures from the World Federation of Exchanges, at the end of 2010 the market capitalisation of its 52 member stock exchanges was an astonishing $57 trillion (that is $57,000,000,000,000 or $8,142 per person with the amount of shares traded in the year valued at $25 trillion.

Figure 6.1 details the relative size of stock markets around the world according to the total market capitalisation of the companies traded on them. Unfortunately the data does not separate China which is a growing financial force (it is part of the 18.5% in the 'Other' category).

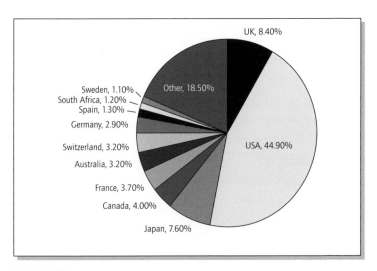

Figure 6.1   Relative sizes of global stock markets by market capitalisation

Source: Elroy Dimson, Paul Marsh and Mike Staunton, Credit Suisse Global Investment Returns Sourcebook 2012

The world has changed dramatically in the last 30 years. Liberalisation and the accelerating wave of privatisation pushed stock markets to the forefront of developing countries' tools of economic progress. The strong communist ideological opposition to capitalism has been replaced with stock markets in Moscow, Warsaw and Sofia.

China has two major thriving stock exchanges, in Shanghai with about 900 companies, and in Shenzhen with over 1,100 companies. There are now tens of millions of Chinese investors who can only be properly described as 'capitalists' given that they put at risk their savings on the expectations of a reward on their capital.

Shifts in stock exchanges

Some exchanges have been amalgamated with larger ones; the London Stock Exchange, LSE, merged with the Borsa Italiana in 2007; the NYSE merged in 2006 with the Euronext group, itself a merger of the Paris, Amsterdam, Brussels and Lisbon exchanges, and in 2008 with the American Stock Exchange. So we now have NYSE Euronext.

The US market with a particular focus on hi-tech firms, NASDAQ, merged in 2007 with OMX, the Scandanavian and Baltic group of exchanges (Stockholm, Helsinki, Copenhagen and Iceland, and Estonia, Latvia, Lithuania and Armenia) and also with the Boston and Philadelphia exchanges, with the result that NASDAQ OMX is the largest US electronic exchange, listing over 2,700 companies in the USA and another 778 in Europe.

To give you some idea of relative size of share trading on the main markets, Table 6.1 provides some data (note that most markets also trade bonds and other securities).

Table 6.1   The world's 20 largest stock exchanges at the end of 2010

	Domestic equities market capitalisation ($ million)	Total share trading in year ($ million)	Number of listed companies Total	Domestic	Foreign
NYSE Euronext (US)	13,394,082	17,795,600	2,317	1,799	518
NASDAQ OMX	3,889,370	12,659,198	2,778	2,480	298
Tokyo SE Group	3,827,774	3,787,952	2,293	2,281	12
London SE Group	3,613,064	2,741,325	2,966	2,362	604
NYSE Euronext (Europe)	2,930,072	2,018,077	1,135	983	152
Shanghai SE	2,716,470	4,496,194	894	894	NA
Hong Kong Exchanges	2,711,316	1,496,433	1,413	1,396	17
TSX Group (Canada)	2,170,433	1,368,954	3,741	3,654	87
Bombay SE	1,631,830	258,696	5,034	5,034	NA
National Stock Exchange India	1,596,625	801,017	1,552	1,551	1
BM&FBOVESPA (Brazil)	1,545,566	868,813	381	373	8
Australian SE	1,454,491	1,062,650	1,999	1,913	86
Deutsche Börse	1,429,719	1,628,496	765	690	75
Shenzhen SE	1,311,370	3,572,529	1,169	1,169	0
SIX Swiss Exchange	1,229,357	788,361	296	246	50
BME Spanish Exchanges	1,171,625	1,360,910	3,345	3,310	35
Korea Exchange	1,091,911	1,607,247	1,798	1,781	17
NASDAQ OMX Nordic Exchange	1,042,154	750,279	778	752	26
MICEX (Russia)	949,149	408,078	250	249	1
Johannesburg SE	925,007	340,025	397	352	45

Source: World Federation of Exchanges: www.worldexchanges.org

A fair market

Would you be willing to put your hard-earned savings into shares quoted on a stock exchange that is not perceived as well run? Of course not. To attract you and other investors, it cannot be a place where some investors, brokers, fund raisers or financiers are in a position to profit unfairly at the expense of other participants. This means, for instance, that insider dealing is prohibited: that is, company officers or others with private knowledge about a company should not use that knowledge to trade in the company's shares.

You also want brokers to be well regulated so that they act in the interest of investors and so that market makers follow strict codes of behaviour. Markets need to be well regulated to avoid abuses, negligence and fraud in order to reassure investors who put their savings at risk. (There is more on regulation in Chapter 18). Markets should also be places where it is reasonably cheap to carry out transactions.

Furthermore, you need information on companies and share price activity. Thus well-run stock exchanges insist on minimum standards of information-flow from companies and help disseminate company announcements. They also publish prices at which trading occurred and other relevant data such as volume of trades.

In addition, a large number of buyers and sellers are likely to be needed for the efficient price setting of shares and to provide sufficient liquidity, allowing you to sell at any time without affecting the market price. It would be awful if the shares you hold only traded once a week. Then, when you want to sell, the market maker or potential buyer will offer worse prices than if there were thousands of shares traded every day.

The main benefits of a well-run stock exchange

Firms can find funds and grow

Because investors in financial securities with a stock market quotation are assured that they are able to sell their shares quickly, cheaply and with a reasonable degree of certainty about the price, they are willing to supply funds to firms at a lower cost than they would if selling was slow, or expensive, or the sale price was subject to much uncertainty. Thus stock markets encourage investment by *mobilising savings*.

Allocation of capital

An efficiently functioning stock market is able to assist in the allocation of investment capital. If the stock market were poorly regulated and operated then the mispricing of shares and other financial securities could lead to scarce capital resources being put into sectors which were inappropriate. If, for instance, the market priced the shares of a badly managed company in a declining industrial sector at a high level, then that firm would find it relatively easy to sell shares and raise funds for further investment in its business or to take over other firms. Companies with better prospects and with a greater potential would be deprived of essential finance.

Stock markets have been great at shifting savings from horse and buggy companies to car producers in the 1910s; from typewriters firms to computer manufacturers in the 1990s; and from vacuum tube makers to flat screen fabricators in the 2000s. All of these were led by shifts in consumer demand as new technology was developed.

For shareholders

As a shareholder you benefit from the availability of a speedy, cheap secondary market if you want to sell. Not only may you like to know that you can sell shares easily, you may simply want to know the value of your holdings without any intention of selling. By contrast, an unquoted firm's shareholders often find it very difficult to assess the value of their holding.

Status and publicity

The public profile of a firm can be enhanced by being quoted on an exchange. Banks and other financial institutions generally have more confidence in a quoted firm and therefore are more likely to provide funds at a lower cost. Their confidence is raised because the company's activities are now subject to detailed scrutiny. Also, the publicity surrounding the process of gaining a quotation may have a positive impact on the image of the firm in the eyes of customers, suppliers and employees and so may lead to a beneficial effect on their day-to-day business.

Mergers

Mergers can be facilitated better by a quotation. This is especially true if the payments offered to the target firm's shareholders for their holdings are shares in the acquiring firm. A quoted share has a value defined by the market, whereas shares in unquoted firms are difficult to assess.

Improves corporate behaviour

If a firm's shares are traded on an exchange, the directors may be encouraged to behave in a manner more conducive to share-holders' interests. This is achieved through a number of pressure points. For example, to obtain a quotation, companies are required to disclose far more information than is required by accounting standards or the Companies Acts. This information is then dissem-inated widely and can become the focus of much public and press comment. In addition, investment analysts ask for regular briefings from senior managers and continuously monitor the performance of firms. Rigorous standards are required from firms wishing to be listed.

The London Stock Exchange (LSE)

The London Stock Exchange (LSE) is probably the most famous stock exchange in the world. While it started over 200 years ago, a significant shift of gear happened in the 1980s, called 'Big Bang'.

Big Bang

Before the Big Bang in 1986, brokers and other market service providers organised share and other security trading such that there was little competition, commission rates were kept high and trading was done on a face-to-face basis. It was a very comfortable existence, until it was threatened by the new types of trading developed in the USA. It became clear in the 1970s and 1980s that the LSE was losing trade to overseas stock markets. For the LSE to remain competitive in the modern world, complacency had to be banished and changes had to happen.

Big Bang is the term used for a collection of reforms that resulted in fixed broker commissions disappearing, foreign competitors being allowed to own member firms (market makers or brokers), the screen-based computer system of trading replacing floor-based face-to-face trading and the LSE becoming a limited company.

The market makers and brokers quickly passed into the hands of large financial conglomerates. Commissions fell sharply for large orders (from 0.4% to around 0.2% of the value traded). Brokers started to specialise; some would offer the traditional service of advice and dealing, whereas others would offer a no-frills dealing-only service, 'execution-only' (see Chapter 4).

Recent moves

In response to demand, in 1995 the LSE launched another market. This was and is for smaller companies, the Alternative Investment Market (AIM). After centuries of being an organisation owned and run by its members, in 2001 the LSE became a public limited company with its shares traded on its own Main Market. It has come a long way from its clubby days.

In 2004, the Stock Exchange moved from its historic site in Old Broad Street to Paternoster Square near St Paul's Cathedral, but it no longer has the focal point of a trading floor – just a bunch of offices. The Exchange toyed with the idea of moving out of the City but decided that its identity is tied too closely to the Square Mile to move outside, and the proximity of other professionals in the same area was too convenient.

The focus of this book is shares, but it is important to note that the LSE is a leading market place for many types of financial securities other than UK shares, including many types of debt securities (e.g. lending to the UK government (gilts), or companies (corporate bonds) or preference shares (see Chapter 8) or shares in foreign companies).

The London Stock Exchange primary market

Through its primary market in listed securities, the LSE has succeeded in encouraging large sums of money to flow annually to firms wanting to invest and grow. On its different markets, it has over 2,900 companies quoted with a total market value of over £4 trillion (i.e. four million million).

The vast majority of these companies raised funds by selling shares, bonds or other financial instruments through the LSE, either when they first floated or by issuing further shares in subsequent years. For example, newly listed UK firms on LSE's Main Market raised new capital by selling over £9bn of shares in 2011. Another £2.5bn was raised by already listed firms selling shares through further issues of equity and by selling other securities such as bonds in pounds sterling.

Over 1,100 companies are on the AIM. These companies, too, have raised precious funds to assist growth – in 2011 this was £3.66bn. The Main Market (Official List) includes hundreds of foreign companies as well as over 1,000 UK companies. These are said to have a *full listing* (unlike AIM companies, which are *quoted*).

At the same time as raising fresh capital, companies transfer money the other way by, for example, paying back money borrowed through bonds, paying interest on debt or dividends on shares. Nevertheless, it is clear that large sums are raised for companies through the primary market.

Each year there is great interest and excitement inside dozens of companies as they prepare for flotation. Since 1999, there have been almost 900 new admissions on the Main Market and over 2,000 on the AIM; these issues have raised billions for the companies involved.

Stringent conditions for joining

The LSE imposes strict criteria for joining the Main Market. The *listing particulars* (*prospectus*) should give a complete picture of the company; its trading history, financial record, management and business prospects.

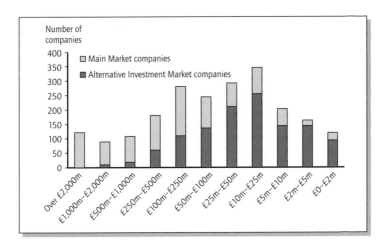

Figure 6.2   **Distribution of UK companies by equity market value 2011**

Source: London Stock Exchange factsheets

It should (normally) have at least a three-year trading history and has to make at least 25% of its ordinary shares publicly available. 'Public' means people or organisations not associated with the directors or major shareholders. It is thought that 25% is needed to allow a sufficient volume of trade to make the shares liquid, enabling shares to change ownership speedily, at low cost and without large movements in price.

Given the costs associated with gaining a listing (often much more than £500,000), it may be surprising to find that the total value of the ordinary shares of the majority of quoted companies is less than £250m (see Figure 6.2). The average market capitalisation of AIM companies is under £25m.

The secondary markets

You are able to buy or sell shares during the 'trading hours', which are between 08.00 and 16.30 Monday to Friday.

Just to give you some background to indicate how liquid the market is with vast amounts of shareholder-to-shareholder trading, I thought I'd provide you with LSE's trading statistics. In a typical month, over 12,000,000 *bargains* (trades between buyers and sellers) are struck between investors in shares on the LSE, worth over £100bn. The size of bargains varies enormously, from £500 trades by private investors to millions by the major funds.

So active is the secondary market that the amount raised in the primary equity market in a year is about the same as the value of shares that trade hands daily in the secondary market, ensuring a liquid market.

The Alternative Investment Market (AIM)

The driving philosophy behind the AIM is to offer young and developing companies access to new sources of finance, while providing investors with the opportunity to buy and sell shares in a trading environment which is run, regulated and marketed by the LSE. Efforts are made to keep the costs down and make the rules as simple as possible.

There is a long-recognised need for equity capital by small, young companies which are unable to afford the costs of full listing. Many stock exchanges around the world have alternative equity markets that set less stringent rules and regulations for joining or remaining quoted (often called *second-tier markets*).

Lightly regulated markets have a continuing dilemma. If the regulation is too lax, scandals of fraud or incompetence will arise, damaging their image and credibility and thus reducing the flow of investor funds to companies. This happened to the German market for small companies, *Neuer Markt*, which had to close in 2002 because of the loss in investor confidence. On the other hand, if the market is too tightly regulated, with more company investigations, more information disclosure and a requirement for longer trading track records prior to flotation, the associated costs and inconvenience will deter many companies from seeking a quotation.

In contrast to the Main Market, there is no requirement for AIM companies to have been in business for a minimum three-year period or for a set proportion of their shares to be in public hands – if they wish to sell only 1–5% of the shares to outsiders then that is OK. They do not have to ensure that 25% of the shares are in public hands.

However, investors have some degree of reassurance about the quality of companies coming to the market. These firms have to appoint, and retain at all times, a *nominated adviser* and *nominated broker*. The nominated adviser, the *nomad*, is selected by the company from a Stock Exchange approved register and they act as a 'quality controller', confirming to the LSE that the company has complied with the rules. Unlike with Main Market companies, there is no pre-vetting of admission documents (prospectus) when it joins, as a lot of weight is placed on the nomad's investigations and informed opinion about the company.

Nominated brokers have an important role to play in bringing buyers and sellers of shares together. Investors in the company are reassured that at least one broker is ready to help shareholders to trade. They also represent the company to investors (a kind of PR role).

The adviser and broker are to be retained throughout the company's life on the AIM. They have high reputations, and it is regarded as a very bad sign if either of them abruptly refuses further association with a firm.

AIM companies, like Main Market companies, are expected to comply with strict rules regarding the publication of any information that may affect the share price and abide by high quality rules for the annual and interim reports. There are some tax advantages of investing in AIM shares – see LSE's website or Chapter 17.

PLUS

PLUS is a stock exchange based in London, and is used by companies that do not want to pay the costs of a flotation on one of the markets run by the LSE (this can range from £100,000 to £1m, even for AIM). Companies quoted on PLUS provide a service to their shareholders, allowing them to buy and sell shares at reasonable cost. It also allows the company to gain access to capital, for example, by selling more shares to investors, without submitting to the rigour and expense of a quotation on LSE.

Note that the criteria for companies gaining admission for a quote do not include compliance with the strict rules set down by the regulator, the UK Listing Authority (see Chapter 14), so investors have far fewer quality assurances about these companies. So, be careful!

Also, the secondary market can be relatively illiquid for the PLUS-quoted securities, with the total number of transactions in a typical month for all 150 or so companies at around 1,000–2,000. Indeed the market makers' bid–offer spread on PLUS shares can be 50% or more. So shareholders need to be wary, but it is better than no secondary market at all.

PLUS companies are generally small and often brand new, but there are also some long-established and well-known firms, such as Thwaites and Adnams. So if you fancy the idea of owning shares in a local beer company PLUS may be the place to go.

Many companies gain a quotation on PLUS without raising fresh capital simply to allow a market price to be set. If no money is raised, no formal admission document or prospectus is required, but the Corporate Adviser (to be retained by the company at all times) will insist that good accounting systems are in place with annual audited accounts and semi-annual accounts. The Corporate Adviser will also ensure that the company has at least one non-executive director, and adequate financing.

Sifting out the important stuff on the internet

Getting information off the Internet is like taking a drink from a fire hydrant.

Mitch Kapor

The internet has been a great boon for investors looking to gather information and it is very handy for trading shares. In the past 15 years, there has been a revolution in the way investors discover key data about a company and select shares. Prior to the online delivery of information, traders had to write to or phone a company to get a copy of the annual report; charts of share prices were only for those in the City* with a Reuters screen; it took an age for company announcements to trickle through.

Today, a quick online search delivers company reports going back 10 years or more as well as an astounding array of stock market statistics on companies: from when directors bought shares in their own companies to share price histories to bulletin board discussions about the company's latest product. In fact, there is so much out there now that there is a danger of being overwhelmed. This chapter will help you sift out the important stuff.

---

* The financial district in London is known as the City – its heart is where the Romans first settled, roughly one square mile from Tower Bridge to St Pauls.

What the company puts out

The place to start is the website of the company you are interested in. There are two aspects to this.

1 How do they present themselves on the internet and what can you glean about the underlying business strengths in terms of customer appeal, etc.;

2 The financials: i.e. how have they been performing with regard to making profits for shareholders? And how strong is the financial structure, e.g. do they have too much debt and are therefore too risky?

Figure 7.1 shows Rolls-Royce's opening page. You can immediately gather important information. If you click on the buttons for its different divisions, such as 'Civil Aerospace', you can get more detailed information on the engines it supplies. Thus a potential customer can read about the spec for a Trent700 engine or one of the other engines it produces.

You can gain a feel for the quality of the company's communication efforts at this point as well as gain some insight into its competitive position benchmarked against other players in the industry. Of course, you are reading a cleaned-up PR version, and so a reasonable amount of scepticism is required but, by combining this information with material from other sources, you can start to build a picture.

A good antidote to corporate PR is to search the company name or their brand products and adding the word 'reviews' to see what customers thought of them. If a lot of them are upset with the company you may decide to pass on this investment.

With Rolls-Royce, the investor information is displayed on the home page so you can click through to the investor section containing news stories of interest to investors as well as annual reports and stock market data such as Rolls Royce's share price.

Other companies, particularly those with a high consumer focus, e.g. Vodafone and Marks & Spencer, have websites mostly concerned with selling products or an image of the firm to the

Figure 7.1   Roll-Royce's home page

Source: www.rolls-royce.com

public. Simply searching using the company name you may find it difficult to discover the material directed at investors. To get there more directly, I usually search on 'investor relations'.

Newspaper websites

Many broadsheet newspapers supply articles free to anyone who visits their websites and you will be able to search for articles going back many years. The most sought-after financial papers, the *Financial Times* and the *Wall Street Journal*, allow you access to many parts of their sites for free but restrict your ability to search their archive of articles to only a limited number of articles in any given period. If you want more you will have to subscribe.

Financial websites

Financial and trading websites will allow you to see market prices for shares 15 minutes after the deal was struck. It is also possible to get a glance at a real-time price (only a few seconds after the deal was struck) for a minute or two, but to get access to 'always-on' real-time prices you have to pay a small monthly fee.

These are some of the players in the business – consult their websites for current services:

www.uk.advfn.com	ADVFN
www.digitallook.com	Digital Look
www.hemscott.com	Hemscott
www.iii.co.uk	Interactive Investor
www.londonmoneymarket.com	London Money Market
www.londonstockexchange.com	London Stock Exchange
www.moneyam.com	Moneyam
www.fool.co.uk	Motley Fool
www.proquote.net	ProQuote
www.tdwaterhouse.co.uk	T.D. Waterhouse
www.finance.yahoo.com	Yahoo! Finance

These websites offer much more than share prices. You can learn a tremendous amount about a company by visiting the sites. Furthermore, you do not have to limit yourself to using just one. By registering with half a dozen (taking two or three minutes for each) you can access an even wider range of information. The only downside is they will send you junk mail – frequently.

Financial website navigation, step by step

Figure 7.2 shows the home page of ADVFN. Other websites have similar features, with some better than others on particular aspects. I'm not promoting ADVFN; I just need to make use of one of the major suppliers to illustrate the amazing range of information available.

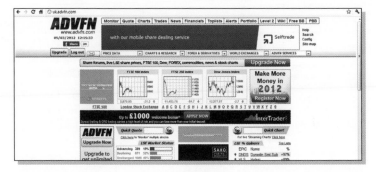

Figure 7.2   The home screen for ADVFN

Source: www.uk.advfn.com

After logging in you may want to look up the price of a particular share. To do this click on the 'Quote' button – top left of screen, shown in Figure 7.3.

Figure 7.3   Home screen with a focus on the 'navigation bar' showing quote button

Source: www.uk.advfn.com

The page that this takes you to allows you to search for a particular company – see Figure 7.4.

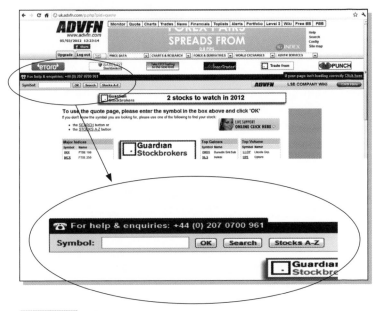

Figure 7.4   **The quote page**

Source: www.uk.advfn.com

Operators in the markets (brokers, etc.) reduce the name of companies down to very short *stock symbols* or *codes*. They are also called *tickers* (particularly in the USA) and *TIDM* codes (they used to be called *EPIC* codes). We'll just call them codes.

So, for example, Rolls-Royce is reduced to RR. and Marks & Spencer to MKS. Most of us do not know the codes that we need, but we can look them up. On the quote page if you click on 'STOCKS A–Z' a screen similar to that in Figure 7.5 will appear. (An alternative is to put, say, Rolls Royce in the 'Symbol' box which will give some choices – but with this route you have to make sure you click on the Rolls-Royce for the LSE. Going the longer route that I will describe means that you end up looking at the Rolls-Royce shares quoted in London and not those in dollars in New York, or even a different company altogether with a similar name.)

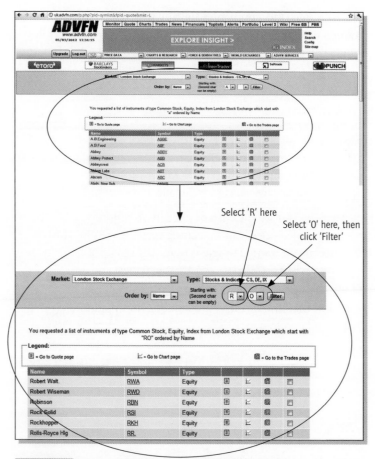

Figure 7.5   Searching for a company (or index) page

Source: www.uk.advfn.com

Make sure that the correct market is being searched – on this screen the default setting is for the LSE (you can look at shares on dozens of markets around the world). Also check that the type of security is the one you want – in this case 'Stocks and indices' is correct (rather than, say, futures, options or bonds).

The buttons on the right permit us to search an alphabetical list. Where it says 'A' we put in 'R', and in the next box 'O', because these are the start of Rolls. Then click on 'Filter'. The results are shown on the lower part of Figure 7.5.

All the quoted LSE companies starting with RO are shown on the screen, starting with Robert Walters. Scroll down to Rolls Royce where you can see the code: RR. The dot is important, it is part of the code.

Prices

Now we are getting somewhere. If you click on the 'RR.' you will get some information on Rolls-Royce as you are taken to the quote page for the company – see Figure 7.6 for the top part of the page. There is a lot on this page, so we'll take it in stages.

▓ First you can see the current price information. There is the latest traded price 'Cur' (meaning current) at 819p. The bid price, if you wanted to sell, is 819p. The offer price, if you are a buyer, is 819.5p. Also shown are the highest and lowest prices for that day.

▓ Below that line we have fundamental information on the

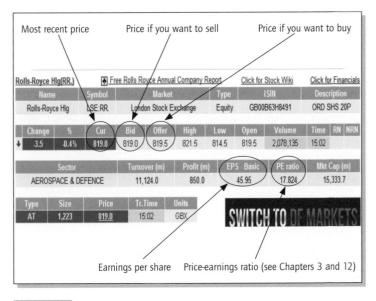

Figure 7.6 Quote page for Rolls-Royce

Source: www.uk.advfn.com

company: its latest reported turnover (how much it sold in a year), profit in millions (this may be out of date – check company accounts for an update), earnings per share (EPS), price to earnings (PE) ratio and market capitalisation (Mkt Cap) as discussed in Chapter 6.

▪ The final line has the most recent trade to go through, showing that it was an automatic trade (AT) through the LSE computers (see Chapter 5), the number of shares (1,223), price (819p), time (15:02) and currency (GBX–UK pounds).

News

All the financial websites supply company announcements and other news. On ADVFN this is displayed on the quote page for Rolls-Royce in a 'Recent News' section – see Figure 7.7. You can see this by scrolling down the quote page.

Clicking on the headline will bring up the full news story. The system carries news and announcements going back many years. So, for example, if you wanted to find out if periodic director statements on the progress of company proved to be accurate or generally over-optimistic you can read both the statements going back ten or more years and read the subsequent reported results.

Recent News			
Date	Time	Source	Headline
02/03/2012	11:47	UKREG	Director/PDMR Shareholding
01/03/2012	15:41	UKREG	Director/PDMR Shareholding
29/02/2012	09:12	UKREG	Total Voting Rights
29/02/2012	09:08	UKREG	Director/PDMR Shareholding
28/02/2012	14:52	UKREG	Annual Information Update
24/02/2012	09:11	UKREG	Annual Financial Report
22/02/2012	15:55	UKREG	Director/PDMR Shareholding
Set a News Alert for RR.			More RR. News

Figure 7.7 Obtaining news on the company – an ADVFN screen

Source: www.uk.advfn.com

Bulletin boards

By scrolling down the quote screen for Rolls-Royce, you can see the message/discussion board or *bulletin board* – see Figure 7.8. This can be an important source of information. The entries are written by anyone registered with the website. Through these, it is

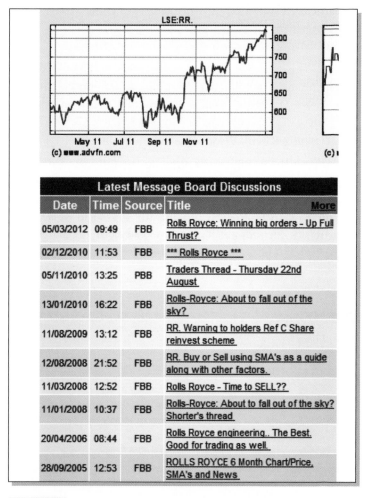

Figure 7.8   A discussion board (ADVFN is shown as an example)

Source: www.uk.advfn.com

possible to correspond with like-minded investors – which helps to make the game of investing less lonely as well as exposing you to alternative views.

People that post on these 'threads' usually adopt nicknames. Some of these individuals are well informed and can add to your knowledge of the company; but beware, others know little, are trying to ramp up or push down a share, or are there just for a rant. Be particularly wary of those who claim they know a takeover bid is coming or the directors are about to sell a large chunk of shares or they have some other inside information. They are trying to get a share price movement so that they can make money for themselves. If they really had this inside knowledge do you think they would share it with you? And anyway insider dealing is illegal.

Tip: it is worth looking at a number of website discussion boards to help build up background knowledge.

Some websites have both free bulletin boards and a premium service that you have to pay to join. ADVFN offer the 'premium' version (the button to click on is at the top of each page 'PBB'). These tend to attract more serious investors.

The most active bulletin boards are:

www.advfn.com	ADVFN
www.hemscott.com	Hemscott
www.moneyam.com	MoneyAM
www.iii.co.uk	Interactive Investor

Financial data

At the top right of the quote page is *Click for Financials* – see Figure 7.9.

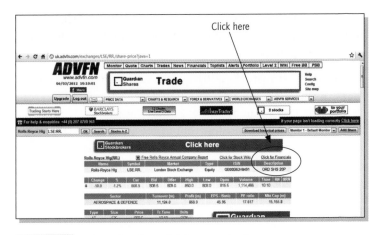

Figure 7.9 Obtaining financial data on the firm

Source: www.uk.advfn.com

By clicking through to this page you have access to a very long list of key financial numbers including a wide range of financial ratios, profit numbers and balance sheet numbers going back four

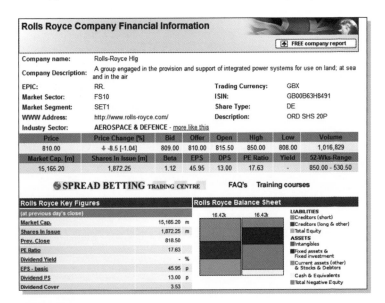

Figure 7.10 Company financial information presented on ADVFN

Source: www.uk.advfn.com

years, share price performance over various periods, a share chart and dividend history going back many years. Figure 7.10 shows the start of the page.

A particularly useful feature on this page is the *more like this* button which will take you to a list of companies in the same industry on the LSE. It is always important for an investor to be aware of the relative strengths of competitor firms. By following the links, you can discover a wide range of information about *some* of the companies that compete.

In the case of Rolls-Royce this does not quite work: you need to take a more international perspective because its main competitors are not quoted on LSE, that is General Electric and Pratt and Whitney.

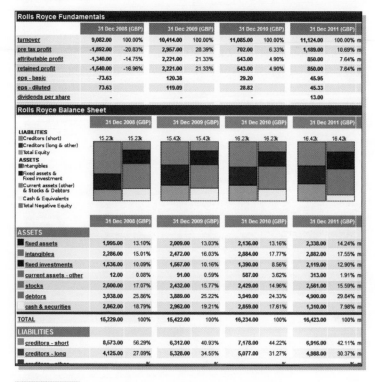

Figure 7.11 Some of the accounting data on ADVFN

Source: www.uk.advfn.com

We do not have space in this book to discuss all the different financial ratios and measures displayed on a page like this, but I will show you the key balance sheet and profit numbers – see Figure 7.11 – these are discussed in Chapters 11 and 12.

Monitoring

Going back to the home screen for ADVFN (Figure 7.2) you can see a string of buttons going across the top – see Figure 7.12.

| Monitor | Quote | Charts | Trades | News | Financials | Toplists | Alerts | Portfolio | Level 2 | Wiki | Free BB | PBB |

Figure 7.12 The main buttons to click

Source: www.uk.advfn.com

The 'Monitor' button allows you to track a number of companies and indices – see Figure 7.13. Once a company is on your monitor list you merely click on the company name to obtain more detail, without having to look up its code. You can also see if there is any recent news about the companies on the list. To add companies to the list just find the relevant code.

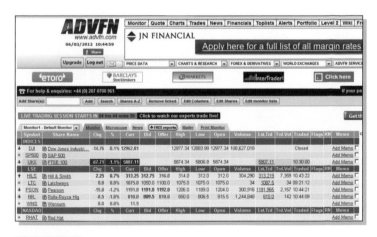

Figure 7.13 Monitoring a select group

Source: www.uk.advfn.com

You can have numerous monitor tables: perhaps you would like one that is focused on, say, retail companies and another one on low PE ratio shares.

Share price charts

The 'Charts' button at the top of the home page allows you to draw share price charts – see Figure 7.14. You can draw charts for various time periods, e.g. for the current day with one minute intervals, or you could go back a couple of decades or more.

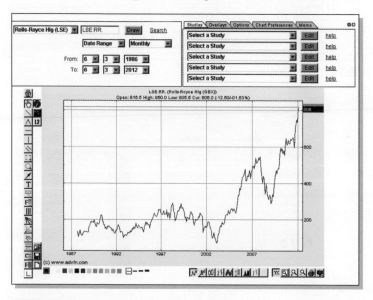

Figure 7.14 A share price chart for Rolls-Royce

Source: www.uk.advfn.com

It is great fun to have a play with these. The websites are usually very responsive so you can try out all sorts of things, such as a chart of moving averages of the share price, rates or change or volume of shares bought by investors.

A history of trades

The next button along (in Figure 7.12), 'Trades', allows you to see the actual deals that have been made in the market. As you can see in Figure 7.15, there is a trade in RR every few seconds at least – in the second at 11:07:51 there were four trades, amounting to almost 2,000 shares sold. Other (much smaller) companies may go days without a single trade. It is possible to see the trades of days past as well as the current day.

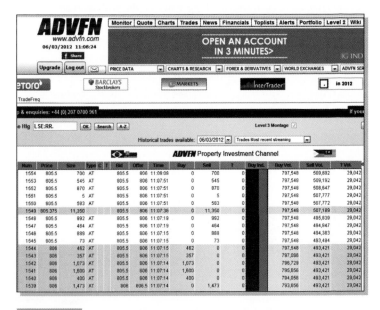

Figure 7.15 A history of trades in the company's shares

Source: www.uk.advfn.com

News

The 'News' button brings you to a page displaying the major news stories of the day, e.g. a merger bid. By inputting the code for the company in which you have an interest you can see all the past announcements, etc.

An alternative use for the 'News' button is to get a continuous stream of news as it is released from all companies on the market – this is constantly updated as you look at it. Most of these announcements are made between 7am and 8 am so, if you are keen on acting on the latest news, you need to get up early. Despite only reporting news from those companies with an important announcement that day, the list of stories is very long.

Toplists

The 'Toplists' button is a great way of selecting, from all the shares on the market, a shortlist of companies based on key criteria, e.g. those that have produced the best or the worst five-year returns. You can then filter out those that, say, were unprofitable last year, or those with a market capitalisation greater than, say, £100m, and so on. This is powerful stuff. You can start off with a list of over 2,000 companies and narrow down to a shortlist of 20 or so that match the investment criteria you set. Figure 7.16 shows only some of the factors that can be used to rank and separate companies.

You can use a variety or combinations of filters. To illustrate, in Figure 7.17 I first selected on the basis of dividend yield. So I now have over 2,200 companies listed in order of the yield. The top of

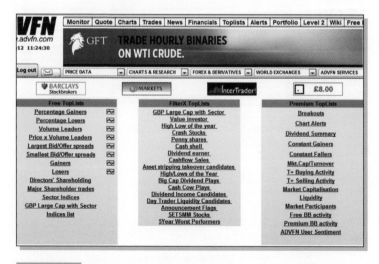

Figure 7.16 Filtering and ranking companies on the markets – 'toplists'

Source: www.uk.advfn.com

page one of the list is shown. To put the companies in order of dividend yield, I clicked on *Div Yield*. There are some amazingly high dividend yields here on page one of the list – the market will be expecting many of these companies to stop paying dividends and thus the share price is pushed down.

If I'm only interested in those companies with dividend yields between 4% and 6% (around page 3 on the list) and which have a PE less than, say, 10, I can add another column very quickly. I click on *Key Figures* and scroll down to PE and click on it. Then I get the new column of numbers headed *PE* alongside the dividend yield column.

I could keep going in this vein, but I've stopped after adding pre-tax profits. This might be because I'm only interested in those firms that have positive profits as well as good dividend yields and low PE ratios.

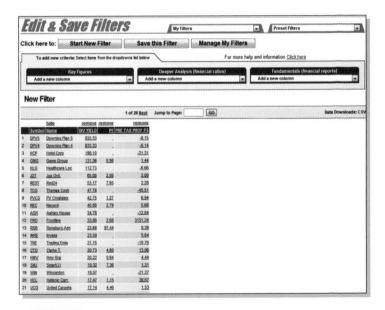

Figure 7.17 An example of filtering, with three criteria

Source: www.uk.advfn.com

Alerts

The 'Alerts' button (Figure 7.12) permits you to program the system to tell you if a particular threshold is reached, e.g. the share price of M&S falls below £2.00.

There are three types of alerts: share price alerts, news alerts and bulletin board alerts. In each case, you can ask the financial website to send you an e-mail message when a particular event occurs.

Creating real and virtual portfolios

The 'Portfolio' button (Figure 7.12) allows you to set up a number of hypothetical or real portfolios and then follow the shares through time. Figure 7.18 shows that the portfolio gains and losses are totalled automatically. You can click through from the company names in the portfolio list to more detailed information on the company.

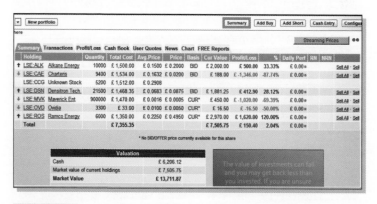

Figure 7.18 A portfolio screenshot

Source: www.uk.advfn.com

You can create as many portfolios as you want. So you might want to follow the performance of shares with low PE ratios and set up a series of such portfolios every six months and follow their progress over the subsequent years. Or you might like to set the system to follow the progress of companies selected on the basis of the investment principles of Warren Buffett.

When checking your portfolio, beware of the psychological problem we humans have when it comes to what behaviouralists call 'narrow framing'. In this context, we lose sight of the bigger investment picture and feel pain as a result. On any one day or month there is a roughly 50:50 chance that your portfolio will be up or down. It turns out that we humans feel a loss much more keenly than a gain.

So if we are continually looking to see whether we have made money in the past few hours or lost it, we will suffer the pain of loss regularly and this will outweigh the pleasure we feel on up-days. This can lead to some bad decisions as we go on a desperate search for short-term fixes to feel the pleasure of a gain.

Do not narrow frame – see the bigger picture, which is that shares generally give a satisfactory return over a number of years, but there will be many bumps along the way. Do not be distracted and depressed by the bumps.

Be a long-term investor in good companies. Consider whether it makes sense to look at your portfolio returns every day. Yes, look at company performance and other data relevant to that performance (e.g. technological change in the industry), but not at stock market ups and downs. This is one of the key lessons from great investors Benjamin Graham and Warren Buffett.†

Level 2

Brokers and many financial websites offer *Level 2* (or *Level II*) prices. The 'Level 2' button (Figure 7.12) allows you to see on your computer the orders for shares that other traders are putting into the LSE's system, with prices they are willing to pay or sell for, and the quantity they are willing to trade.

---

† If you would like to know more on sound investment philosophies you might like to read *Great Investors* (FT Prentice Hall, 2011) or *The Financial Times Guide to Value Investing* (FT Prentice Hall, 2009) or join us for a day of investment seminars (*www.glen-arnold-investments.co.uk*).

We saw in Figure 7.6 (page 96) Level 1 data: simply bid and offer prices, price of last trade executed, current day's high and low, percentage change from the previous close of trading, the amount of volume traded and the highest and lowest prices in the last 52 weeks.

Having Level 2 permits a greater understanding of the current supply and demand conditions because it allows the private investor to see the current unfilled buy and sell orders, which can change in front of their eyes as the system continuously streams updates. This provides a better understanding of how the share price is derived and helps in timing the placing of an order. A screenshot of Level 2 prices was shown in Figure 5.1 (page 65), where the trading mechanisms are discussed. The 'direct market access' discussion in Chapter 5 is also relevant here.

Level 2 is useful if you are a regular trader, but for many long-term buy-and-hold investors who trade infrequently it seems quite expensive at £40 or more per month. An all-singing-all-dancing system might cost over £100 per month.

Personally, as a long-term investor, rather than a short-term speculator, I have not yet found a good enough use for Level 2 that will justify the cost. If you think you can do successful short-term in and out trading many times in a year then good luck to you. For those of us with holding horizons of many years and decades, a few fractions of percent off the buying/selling price does not make a huge difference – certainly not hundreds of pounds per year difference to pay for Level 2.

Director's dealings

Another piece of the information jigsaw you might find useful is whether the directors of the company have been buying or selling its shares. Many investors take a purchase as an indicator of a positive opinion of the firm's prospects by someone with superior access to information – if they are spending their own money on the shares, perhaps there is reason to think they might be undervalued. On the other hand, a sale may not be as negative as it first appears – school fees might need to be paid, or rational diversification is taking place: much depends on context.

A good website for director's dealings is *www.moneyam.com* which displays what directors bought/sold, as well as each of their overall holdings, and at what volume. A chart showing buys and sells relative to accounting year-end dates is handy as stronger signals on the company's prospects might be indicated when the directors start to get a feeling for the annual performance – see Figure 7.19.

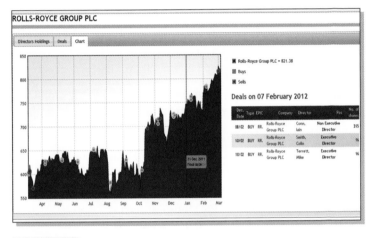

Figure 7.19 Director's dealings shown on a screenshot from Moneyam.com

Source: MoneyAM Limited

Trading online: So how do you actually buy or sell online?

I'll use Charles Stanley's Fastrade web system to illustrate. Figure 7.20 shows that you have £7,231.80 in your account at Charles Stanley to buy shares – you are called Mr Fastrade on this account.

First click whether you want to buy or sell. Then put in the code for the shares – in this case Game, the computer games retailer with the code GMG.L. Now input how many shares you want to buy and whether you would like an 'at market order' or you would like to put an upper limit on the price – see Chapter 4 to understand these orders. Finally, enter your personal secret PIN number and click 'OK'.

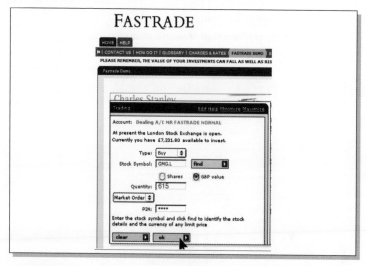

Figure 7.20 Inputting buying instructions – Fastrade's system

Source: www.fastrade.co.uk

After pressing 'OK' the following screen pops up and the clock starts ticking down from 15 seconds – see Figure 7.21.

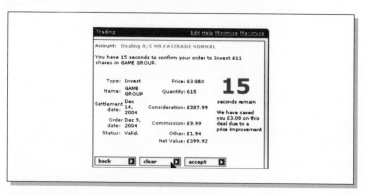

Figure 7.21 The moment of buying page

Source: www.fastrade.co.uk

Don't panic! You do not have to rush into anything. You can let the countdown finish and start the process again without penalty. If, however, you like the details of the deal shown on the screen you can click on the *accept* button.

Now you've done it – you have bought some shares!

8

Preference, foreign and golden shares

An investment in knowledge pays the best interest.

Benjamin Franklin

So far we have only discussed ordinary shares of UK companies. For the most part, these are what UK investors put their money into. However, it might be worth considering preference shares (known as prefs), which offer a route to investment with less risk than ordinary shares but with higher returns than on bonds.

Another alternative is investment in overseas shares. There is logic in not having all your eggs in one economic basket (the UK economy) and spreading your portfolio across a number of countries. Many advanced and emerging economies offer the prospect of rapid development and high share returns. On the other hand, there are dangers of operating in poorly regulated and unfamiliar territory.

I'll round off the chapter with a description of golden shares; which are not as glamorous as they sound.

Preference shares

Preference shares appeal to investors seeking regular stable income as they offer their owners a fixed rate of dividend each year. However, if the firm has insufficient profits the amount paid will be reduced, sometimes to zero, and therefore there is no guarantee that an annual income will be received, unlike with debt capital. Nevertheless, it is rare for a preference dividend to be missed, especially as the dividend on preference shares has to be paid before anything is paid out to ordinary shareholders. In effect, after the preference dividend obligation has been met there may be nothing left for ordinary shareholders.

Preference shares are also attractive because they offer a regular income at a higher rate of return than that available on the alternative of investing in debt securities, say by buying bonds issued by the firm. However, this higher return also comes with higher risk, as the preference dividend ranks for payment after bond interest. So if the firm is going through a rough patch, the bondholders are likely to be paid their interest, but the preference share holders may not receive anything that year. Moreover, if the firm is liquidated (the creditors are insisting that all assets are sold off to pay them back) preference holders are further back in the queue than the debt holders as recipients of the proceeds of the asset sales.

Preference shareholders are not usually able to benefit from any extraordinarily good performance of the firm – any profits above expectations go to the ordinary shareholders. Also preference shares usually carry no voting rights, unless the dividend is in arrears or in the case of a liquidation. Preference shares may be bought through a broker in the same way that you buy ordinary shares.

While it is possible to make capital gains by trading in and out of preference shares they tend to be much less volatile than ordinary shares and generally behave more like bonds responding to interest rate changes.

Why a firm might like to issue preference shares

One of the reasons why companies issue preference shares is that the dividends can be omitted for one or more years. This can give the directors more flexibility and a greater chance of surviving a downturn in trading. Contrast this with debt capital, which carries an obligation to pay interest regardless of the firm's difficulties. Although there may be no legal obligation to pay a dividend every year, the financial community is likely to take a dim view of a firm that missed a dividend – this may have an adverse effect on the price of the ordinary shares as investors become nervous and sell. Also preference shares are an additional source of capital, which, because it does not (usually) confer voting rights, does not dilute the influence of the ordinary shareholders on the firm's direction.

Variations on the theme of preference share

Here are some features that can be added (these words are likely to be in the title of the preference shares you might buy):

- **Cumulative.** If dividends are missed in any year the right to eventually receive a dividend is carried forward. These prior-year dividends have to be paid before any payout to ordinary shareholders.

- **Participating.** As well as the fixed payment, the dividend may be increased if the company has high profits. Participating prefs are rare.

- **Redeemable.** These have a finite life, at the end of which the initial capital investment will be repaid.

- **Irredeemables** (more common) have no fixed redemption date.

- **Convertibles.** These can be converted into ordinary shares at specific dates and on preset terms (e.g. one ordinary share for every two preference shares). These shares often carry a lower yield (dividend as a proportion of share price) since there is the attraction of a potentially large capital gain.

- **Variable rate.** A variable dividend is paid. The rate may be linked to general interest rates or to some other variable factor.

Financial Times

You can see the prices and dividend yields of preference shares quoted in the *Financial Times*, alongside prices of ordinary shares – there are 85 listed in London. For example, Standard Chartered Bank ordinary share price is listed in the *FT*. Below that are its '7.375%Pf' shares and its '8.25%Pf' shares.

The 7.375% prefs are non-cumulative irredeemable preference shares which started off giving an annual dividend which was 7.375% of the amount paid for the shares when first issued. They are bought and sold regularly and so the secondary market price changes. When I looked them up they had risen in price so they were then yielding only 7.33%.

The 8.25% prefs are also non-cumulative irredeemable. By mid-2012, their prices had risen to 117.5p and so they yielded just over 7% rather than 8.25% if you bought them at that point. At 7% this is much better than deposit account interest, but you have to accept that many banks had already stopped paying dividends on ordinary shares and preference shares by this stage in the banking crisis. Because these are non-cumulative you cannot recover lost dividends in future years if Standard Chartered goes through a bad patch and cannot pay. So they come with risk as well.

In 2012, most prefs were offering dividend yields in the range 6–10%, which compared well with the yield on ordinary shares of around 3.7–4%. But bear in mind that ordinary share dividends can 'participate'. That is, as profits rise the dividend is likely to rise, whereas the pref dividend is usually static. Dividends on prefs are normally paid half-yearly.

Unfortunately, there are very few trades in most of the preference shares available, and so it is not always easy for a holder to sell quickly without experiencing a large reduction in price. This makes them very much buy-and-hold investments (for many years).

Overseas shares

UK shares account for about 8% of the value of equities quoted on stock exchanges around the world. Why limit yourself to British companies when there are so many opportunities elsewhere? In the past, the answer to this question from many investors was that trading foreign shares involved more cost, more risk and generally more hassle. Matters have improved dramatically as the internet has made the obtaining of information about overseas companies much easier, as well as allowing online trading.

The intense competition between brokers invading each other's geographic territory has pushed down costs and increased the quality of services. The shift to electronic trading and settlement of share transactions in the majority of developed overseas markets has simplified administration processes enormously. Less paper passing through fewer hands has resulted in lower costs and fewer mistakes. Encouraged by this modernisation, over one-fifth of UK investors have taken the plunge and bought non-UK shares.

Many UK brokers offer access to international markets. Competition in this area is hotting up, particularly for online execution-only trading. In some cases, commissions have fallen to the same level as for dealing in UK shares, but more typically you might pay 1.5–2 times as much, if you include the *foreign currency fee*.

Charges for overseas broking are often raised because of the cost of paying *custodian* fees, that is, paying a broker in the other country to act as a nominee, holding the shares, handling dividends and other administrative activities. Orders placed with your broker are executed directly through the overseas exchange. You can set price limits or instruct your broker to trade *at best* (see Chapter 4).

Your broker is likely to ask you to sign a *Risk Warning Notice* acknowledging that you are aware of additional risks of overseas investment. For US shares there is also a form (W-8BEN) stating your non-US status so that dividends can be paid without the full tax amount usually deducted from that income.

In most developed markets, settlement is three days after the trade, so brokers need access to your money quickly. Therefore they generally insist on the setting up of a *broking account* (a broker cash management account) and nominee account (see Chapter 5). For regular overseas traders it is usually wise to operate with semi-permanent foreign currency accounts in, say, dollars or euros as this will reduce the costs of regular currency conversions.

It is possible to open a foreign currency account and trade through an *overseas broker*. The initial deposit is fairly high at around $10,000, but the internet makes communicating cheap, quick and simple.

UK taxation is payable on income and capital gains from overseas equities in the normal way. However, if *withholding tax* (deducted before a dividend is sent to you, then sent by your company to the tax authorities) has already been charged overseas, as a UK investor you can claim a tax credit to avoid being charged twice. Her Majesty's Revenue and Customs allows any share quoted on a recognised stock exchange to be held in the tax-beneficial individual savings accounts (ISAs) or self-invested personal pensions (SIPPs) (see Chapter 17). Most countries do not impose stamp duty on share purchases.

Points to consider about investing abroad

- Many brokers will only deal in the leading companies in the leading stock markets.
- Shareholder rights are not as well protected in many countries as in the UK. Even some European countries have poor reputations for matters such as protecting small shareholders, openness to takeover, amount of information released and concentration of boardroom power in a clique (families often rule the roost from behind the scenes). Large international businesses tend to be better and follow best international practice.
- Keeping track of medium-sized and small companies can be difficult. Information may not be supplied in English, either by the company or brokers. Newspapers such as the *Financial*

Times cover the large firms, but obviously cannot bring to your attention details about every foreign company. Try the websites *www.adr.com* from J.P. Morgan, *www.quicken.com* and national Yahoo Finance sites.

- You could be exposed to currency shifts. However, if you have investments in a number of currencies you can take a sanguine swings-and-roundabouts attitude to this.

- On the whole, it is still more expensive to buy abroad than at home.

- In the developing world, trading systems may be inefficient: settlement systems often rely on paper, which can be carelessly handled, even lost. Share certificates have been known to arrive months after the transaction. Insider trading and corruption can mean that the outsider is at a considerable disadvantage.

- Political risks – meaning negative consequences as a result of government action, e.g. nationalisation without compensation – are a serious worry in some parts of the world, despite a general shift to international openness and respectability.

- You may have to file a tax return in the relevant country.

Depositary receipts

Alternatives to investing directly in overseas shares include the purchase of *depositary receipts* in foreign companies in your own country. These are certificates which can be bought and sold in the UK which represent evidence of ownership of a company's shares held by a depositary. Thus, an Indian company's shares could be packaged in groups of five by a UK depositary (usually a bank) which then sells a certificate representing the bundle of shares. The depositary receipt can be denominated in a currency other than the corporation's domestic currency and dividends can be received in the currency of the depositary receipt rather than the currency of the original shares. These are attractive securities because they may be more liquid (plenty of trades each day so you can buy or sell without moving the price) and more easily traded than the underlying shares.

They may also be used to avoid settlement, foreign exchange (it may be difficult to obtain the currency) and foreign ownership difficulties (the government might be obstructive to foreigners buying their shares) which may exist in the company's home market. From the company's point of view, depositary receipts are attractive because they allow a market in the company's shares (even though they are wrapped up in a depositary receipt) permitting fund raising and the other benefits of a listing on a regulated global capital market without the company needing to jump the regulatory hurdles necessary to join the Main Market (Official List) in London.

Many foreign companies have depositary receipts traded on the LSE. *American depositary receipts* are available in the USA.

International nature of UK companies

Larger UK companies (e.g. BP, GlaxoSmithKline and Vodafone) derive a large part of their profits from overseas, and so you could gain international exposure by buying UK shares in a UK regulatory environment. So even if the UK economy suffers, companies such as Diageo go on growing as the developing world swigs more Scotch whiskey and Guinness.

Emerging and frontier

Emerging stock markets are those in countries with relatively low/middle incomes but with rapid economic growth, for example China, Indonesia and India, or countries that have reached a fairly high level of income per head but which have small under-developed stock markets and limited internationalisation of financial markets, e.g. many eastern European countries, Turkey and Chile.

The place where the line is drawn between advanced and emerging economies and stock markets is highly subjective. Different researchers use different factors to classify countries, so there are many alternative lists of emerging markets, but the core countries are the BRIC countries: Brazil, Russia, China and India.

Frontier markets are places that have stock markets where you can invest but they tend to be very small with few companies listed. Turnover of shares is generally low and there might be government restrictions placed on your ability to buy into their companies. They are often poor countries such as Kenya, Vietnam and Tanzania.

They are a subset of emerging markets with such low market capitalisations and turnover that they are not included in the larger emerging market indexes. They can be exciting places for you to pick up high-growth companies in high-growth economies at a time when most investors are steering clear. But beware of the extra risk associated with a lower quality legal environment, capricious governments and suspect corporate governance.

Unfortunately, not many UK brokers will buy frontier market shares for you. They simply do not have the systems and overseas contacts in place. As a result, most investors gain exposure to frontier markets by investing through a collective fund such as a unit trust or investment trust. See *The Financial Times Guide to Investing* by Glen Arnold for a description of collective funds.

Some useful websites for investors in overseas shares

Stock exchanges such as the New York Stock Exchange (*www.nyse.com*) have very good websites providing information and links. As well as these you might like to try the following:

www.bloomberg.com	Bloomberg
www.schwab.com	Charles Schwab
www.money.cnn.com	CNN Money
www.corporateinformation.com	Corporate Information
www.digitallook.com	Digital Look
www.edgar-online.com	Edgar Online
www.euroland.com	Euroland
www.ft.com	Financial Times
www.hoovers.com	Hoovers
www.idealing.com	idealing.com

www.internetnews.com	Internet news
www.adr.com	J. P. Morgan
www.reuters.com	Reuters
www.wsj.com	Wall Street Journal
www.tdwaterhouse.co.uk	T. D. Waterhouse

Brokers' websites can provide you with details about their services and supply research tools.

Golden shares

Golden shares are shares with extraordinary special powers, for example the right to block a takeover. The UK government holds golden shares in a number of privatised firms, e.g. BAE Systems and Rolls-Royce. So if you own shares in Rolls-Royce do not expect a takeover from a Russian oligarch with links to the Kremlin; the UK government will stop it.

Golden shares are also useful if a company wishes to preserve certain characteristics it possesses. Football clubs can have golden shares dictating, for example, that 80% of revenues from transfer fees be reinvested in new players (e.g. Nottingham Forest) – but Russian oligarchs are welcomed!

9

What drives share prices?

You get recessions, you have stock market declines. If you don't understand that's going to happen, then you're not ready, you won't do well in the markets.

Peter Lynch

The glib answer to the question of what drives or moves share prices is the weight of supply versus the weight of demand. If large numbers of shareholders are supplying shares to be sold in the stock market while few are demanding shares, then the price will fall. However, we'll need to dig deeper to uncover the factors that lead to increases or decreases in the supply of shares for sale, or to changes in demand.

Business is business, regardless of scale

Imagine that you own a corner shop business in partnership with others. The way you evaluate the viability and valuation of that business is exactly the same way that you would evaluate a company on the stock market. The fundamentals are the same; and those fundamentals are the main drivers of share prices.

So what do you think about when evaluating your corner shop? I suggest that your primary concern will be the flow of income you will receive. As I stated in Chapter 3, this income can come in two forms (leaving aside perks): first, dividends, and second, capital gains.

Now think about where capital gains come from. It is from other investors being willing to pay you more for your shares than you paid, a year or more down the line. Why would they be willing to pay you anything in, say, five years from now? Because they expect to receive dividends from that point forward. If, in turn, they sell later on, then the next buyer in the line will be thinking about future dividends. Even for investors that intend to hold shares for a mere year or two, the most fundamental driver of share prices is the stream of future profits, and therefore dividends, for decades ahead.

A multiplicity of factors

What are the influences on the future flow of income from your corner shop? One key factor is the quantity of assets. Does it have a large or small display area? with plenty of stock or little? We might also be interested in the assets because an alternative to receiving future income is to sell off the assets – perhaps to that property developer who has been making generous offers.

On the flip side of the assets factor, the future profits might be vulnerable because the company has massive liabilities, e.g. a large bank loan relative to the value of assets. If there was a downturn in business or a rise in interest rates, the company would be forced to pay interest regardless, which could reduce profits and in extreme circumstances lead to failure.

Then there is a range of intangible factors influencing the future flow. What is the quality of the competition like? Are the managers highly competent and motivated to produce good returns for shareholders? Does the business have a store of customer goodwill it can draw on?

The corner shop can also be buffeted by the storms in the economy generally. Are we headed for a severe recession? Is the local economy badly affected by the closure of a major employer? Is that caused by changes in exchange rates or government policy?

So, there are company-specific factors that impact on the flow to shareholders and there are market-wide or industry-wide factors. Chapter 10 will look in more detail at the importance of the strengths of the firm relative to the competition and at the factors you need to examine to judge the competence and integrity of the managers. Chapters 11 and 12 will show you how to examine the key numbers produced by the company in its accounts; mostly profits, cash flow, assets and liabilities. While these look at the past of the firm, and we are interested in its future, they give us some clues to help estimate profits and financial stability. That leaves this chapter to concentrate on the wider factors that influence most or all firms, such as the rate of economic growth.

Economic growth

We all know from day-to-day experience that the state of the economy affects our lives. If the economy is booming then jobs are easy to find, house prices are rising and people have increasing amounts of money to spend. On the other hand, in recession many people lose jobs, and may become bankrupt. Even those who are not so badly affected are infected with the general malaise, leading to spending cautiousness and a reduced appetite for risk taking.

Companies are also vulnerable to these ups and downs. When the economy is booming profits tend to rise, they are more inclined to invest and worry less about borrowing and undertaking risky activities. When recession hits, profits tend to fall, and fears of business failure reign. Just ask the shareholders in the once proud Woolworths. If it was not for the slowdown in consumer spending and the stricter credit terms imposed by frightened suppliers it might have survived.

So, clearly the prospects for economic growth over the next year or two will have an impact on the supply and demand for shares.

Great investors often welcome the fear that comes with recession. Their reasoning is that investors tend to over-react to short-term problems. If people like Warren Buffett are analysing a company with a very strong business model they are thinking about the flow of income it will produce over the next 20–30 years, i.e. over many economy-wide ups and downs. If it is a sound business then it will come through the current recession, and may even be stronger because so many of its weaker competitors fall by the wayside (over-borrowed or lacking sufficient strength in the market place). When the majority are frightened and push shares of companies to very low levels on fears of an apocalypse, very selectively the great investors are in there, picking up bargains. However, this is only because they have thoroughly analysed the quality of the firm's 'economic franchise'. I'll give you some tools to analyse along these lines in Chapter 10.

On other occasions, the market can get irrationally exuberant in boom times, pushing shares to ridiculously high levels. One of the great investors, Benjamin Graham, put the tendency of the generality of investors to become excessively fearful or excessively optimistic about either the market as a whole or about a particular share brilliantly with his Mr Market parable*. His main point is that you should not go along with the crowd on whether to buy or sell, but do your own analysis:

Imagine that in some private business you own a small share that cost you $1,000. One of your partners, named Mr. Market, is very obliging indeed. Every day he tells you what he thinks your interest is worth and furthermore offers either to buy you out or to sell you an additional interest on that basis. Sometimes his idea of value appears plausible and justified by business developments and prospects as you know them. Often, on the other hand, Mr. Market lets his enthusiasm or his fears run away with him, and the value he proposes seems to you a little short of silly.

If you are a prudent investor or a sensible businessman, will you let Mr. Market's daily communication determine your view of a $1,000 interest in the enterprise? Only in case you agree with him, or in case you want to trade with him. You may be happy to sell out to him when he quotes you a ridiculously high price, and equally happy to

---

* If you would like to learn more about Benjamin Graham's ideas you could read his book, *The Intelligent Investor* (4th edn, 1973, Harper Business). Alternatively, you might like to join us for a day of seminars looking at his method alongside those of other investors, such as Warren Buffett (see *www.glen-arnold-investments.co.uk*).

buy from him when his price is low. But the rest of the time you will be wiser to form your own ideas of the value of your holdings, based on full reports from the company about its operations and financial position.

B. Graham, The Intelligent Investor

The Eurozone crisis of 2011–12 is an obvious economic event that caused havoc to financial assets around the world. If you can spare the time to read about the causes and effects of such events, you might be able to position yourself to avoid the worst of the trouble – you might even be able to spot opportunities amid the flux.

It takes time to understand economic forces, but all serious investors should start by reading an intelligent newspaper, because good article writers will help to put events in context. Note that I do not recommend that you start by reading economic textbooks, which are really boring, with unnecessary algebraic detail. But you might consult a simple introduction to the key concepts written for the layperson.

Once you understand the context and sequence of consequences of economic events, you might spot warning signs and recovery signs before other people. Books by or on experienced investors or on stock market and economic history are also useful for learning from the mistakes in history – you can't live long enough to make them all yourself!

The level of insightful perspective you gain from reading will allow you to ask questions such as:

- **In 1999:** Are we really in a new era that justifies PE ratios of 40? Is the new technology more revolutionary, leading to unprecedented levels of economic growth, than that of the early twentieth century when electricity, the motor car and medical advances were having an impact?

- **In 2008:** Are house prices getting out of line relative to wages or to rents? What will be the consequences if they fall due to oversupply, for the banks and for consumers who are borrowing heavily?

■ **In 2012:** Can Greece, Italy and Spain really grow their way out of the crisis if governments cut spending?

I try to read the *FT* each day and *The Economist* each week.

GDP

A quick note on a key item of jargon: GDP stands for gross domestic product. It is simply the total of the output of all the nation's people in one year *sold to others* (in addition, there is charitable output, work at home and acts of kindness to family and friends). Thus the value of all the cars manufactured is added to the value of all the fridges manufactured is added to the value of all the haircuts and so on. Basically, what was paid for them. Mature economies reckon they are doing well if they grow the quantity produced by 2.5-3% per year; developing Asian economies reckon that if they produce only 5% more one year than prior year they are doing badly.

To give some perspective, UK annual GDP is around £1,500 billion, USA annual GDP is around $15,000 billion, which is roughly one-fifth of world output.

Inflation and interest rates

Everyone knows that the Bank of England has the power to change interest rates. It normally does this by influencing the banks to alter their *base rates*. This is the rate of interest used by commercial banks as the basis for their lending – a borrower may have a deal to borrow at say, two percentage points over the base rate. The *central banks* (regulatory organisations that control the credit system – e.g. Bank of England, European Central Bank and The Federal Reserve in the USA) may also intervene in those financial markets focused on short-term lending (this is large-scale lending through the financial system).

As we found out in the great recession following 2008, central banks can also opt for *quantitative easing*, which means buying bonds in order to push down interest rates on borrowings for two years or more.

But why do they do it? Their primary motivation is to get the economy moving at the right pace, neither too fast, which might lead to higher inflation, nor too slow, which might lead to prices falling (*deflation*) and lost economic activity and all the misery associated with high unemployment. Thus, if the central bank perceives that inflation over the next year or two will rise too high it might increase interest rates.

The central bank is not the only actor on this stage. For example, rates of interest on bonds issued by the Italian government to be repaid after 10 years rose to over 6% in 2012. Those on Spanish government 10-year bonds were over 7%. Business borrowing was at even higher rates than these. Neither the central bank nor the governments of these countries wanted such high figures. They were caused by the fear of non-payment (*default risk*). In other words bond investors would only lend to these governments if they were compensated very well for the risk of not getting paid.

Why should you, as an equity investor, care about interest rate changes?

- Rising interest rates can send share prices lower because consumers have less to spend (their mortgage and other loan payments rise), therefore the demand for goods and services falls off, reducing profits.
- Other companies suffer greater interest payments because they have high borrowing, therefore they stop buying from your company.
- If your company has a lot of borrowing and interest rates rise, it may be vulnerable to financial failure.
- High interest rates might push up the value of the pound, which depresses the export orders for your company.

Of course, the impact depends on the size of the rise, and on other influences in the economy. So, if the economy is booming anyway, a small rise to slightly dampen demand will not dramatically damage the profit prospects of your company. Context is all when it comes to *macroeconomic†* shifts such as this.

Export potential and currency shifts

If your company exports much of its output it can be badly affected by a rise in the value of its currency. German, Ghanian and Goan customers of your UK manufacturer see price rises of, say, 20% when other potential suppliers have kept prices steady in euros, cedis or rupees. Your company could decide to keep the price constant for its overseas customers in their currencies, but that will result in a 20% cut in amount received in pounds. This could wipe out profits.

Even if your company is British and sells only to UK customers, it might be badly affected by a rise in the pound. Now customers can buy from overseas competitors at lower amounts in pounds.

Change in the industry

There are various changes within an industry which can potentially affect the value of investments.

- There might be news specific to the industry of your company. For example, a rise in the cost of commodities (iron, plastics and oil) leads to a reduced demand for cars and thus a fall in share prices.
- Perhaps a complementary product/service has become cheaper which transforms the fortunes of an industry. For example, the falling cost of tablet computers has encouraged greater sales of online games.
- Alternatively, consumers might be abandoning the industry.

---

† Meaning the large aggregate items in the economy, e.g. the overall growth rate, the national inflation rate, savings rates, exchange rate, government borrowing or level of exports. As opposed to *microeconomic* factors which is more specific at the company level; individual decision units such as firms and consumers determining things like prices of goods, cost of labour and price of land.

Today we are witnessing the hollowing out of the retailers of electrical items such as TVs as consumers switch to cheaper prices on the internet. It only takes a loss of 10% or so of turnover for many shops to become unprofitable.

- Occasionally, we see waves of mergers taking place in an industry, which can push up some shares. On the other hand, investors often worry that the acquirer is paying too much, which pushes down its shares.

Cyclical industries

The demand in some industries fluctuates greatly with the rise and fall of economy. In times of growth the demand for, say, holidays and cars rises disproportionately. However, when the good times come to a shuddering halt, people ask whether they really do need an expensive holiday? Or whether they can postpone the replacement of the car for another year or two? Thus sales of some industries can plummet in hard times.

Defensive industries

There are many goods or services that you and I go on buying even in recession, such as food, medicines and electricity. Thus there are certain points in the economic cycle when defensive shares are pushed up because investors forecast trouble ahead for the cyclical sectors and put their money into the safe haven of defensive industries.

Government actions

Government actions can kill off an otherwise viable company. For example:

- A change in policy on defence supplies can damage an aerospace or armoured vehicle manufacturer.
- Emission prohibitions for cars can pressurise the luxury car sellers.
- The lifting of barriers to foreign companies may lower profits for your firm.

■ A rise in taxes, either generally or more specifically, such as raising petrol duty can kill off many companies.

On the other hand, government actions can boost a company tremendously, e.g. those who take on the work 'outsourced' from government, such as finding the unemployed jobs or running prisons. Other examples include subsidies for solar power or bus transport.

So, you need to keep thinking about the potential for loss of profits or a boost as a result of changes in laws or government policy. How vulnerable is your company to price controls or regulations or new taxes? Is it in a sector that tends to be ignored by politicians and regulators or is it regularly under attack, e.g. tobacco or export of weapons?

Social trends

There are many social trends that impact on the future profits and dividend flow, for example:

■ Increased obesity leads to increased demand for certain types of medicines.

■ People living longer leads to more demand for services catering to the elderly.

■ Life-long learning is a boon for educational suppliers.

The anticipation machine

Don't forget that the market is an anticipation machine. This means that there are thousands of people, some professional, some not, who try to forecast what news about a company or the economy will come out in the next few weeks. They then go into the market to buy or sell on the expectation of their estimates being correct. Thus, share prices move up or down ahead of news announcements, such as increased profits or a massive rise in unemployment.

It sometimes confuses the novice investor that the market

response on the day of the announcement is the opposite of what 'common sense' says it should be. So, if a company announces a doubling of profits, the market newcomer thinks it perverse that the share price falls. The reason is that the market had been expecting a trebling of profits and so had pushed up the price in anticipation. The disappointment results in a flood of sell orders.

Or consider the paradoxical response to news that the economy grew by 5% last year, far greater than previously thought. Investors, like chess players, think a few moves down the line. An excessively hot economy will lead to inflation as wage demands rise and companies push up selling prices – just because they can. This leads to a sharp rise in interest rates which, in turn, leads to reduced demand and output a year or two from now.

Don't do the following

- Trade into investment fads. History is littered with investment fads. Believe it or not, in seventeenth-century Amsterdam the great thing to invest in was tulip bulbs. Some bulbs were so 'valuable' that people would mortgage their houses to buy one bulb. You see, they had heard of friends getting rich by buying a bulb and selling it a few months later. Of course, it ended in tears with bulb prices falling to a fraction of the previous levels. Another highlight (lowlight!) was the railway boom of the nineteenth century. More recently, we have had the dotcom boom, biotechnology and green energy. In my view, the latest batch of companies from Silicon Valley have a faint whiff of the fad about them – speculators are pricing in a heck of a lot of future socialising on websites. They are also expecting a lot of advertising potential.

- Just because prices have shot up in the past year, this form of 'investment' does not become more attractive – it becomes less attractive. So when you see market prices move upward due to a fad, run a mile. Be fearful when others are greedy, and greedy when others are fearful.

- Fall for the gambler's fallacy. If you are tossing a fair coin and it has shown six heads in a row is it more likely that the next toss will show a head or a tail, or are they equally likely? If you answered tail then you are suffering from the gambler fallacy. A run of luck, or bad luck in the past does not influence odds in the future. With a fair coin there is an even chance that the seventh toss will produce a head or a tail. For share investors:

- Don't pay attention to people who say that because a share price has halved it is due for a rise. Statistically, it can halve again, and the past events have no bearing on what is 'due' next. Analysis of the business may, however, lead to a conclusion that the odds are on the side of an eventual rise.

- Newspapers often say the market is in an up (bullish) phase or a down (bearish) phase, suggesting that the probabilities of future movements are stacked one way or the other. These are no more than assertions, not evidence or reliable predictions. The great investors say they do not have a clue where the stock market is going over the next 6–12 months. And yet, all those commentators on the TV and in papers, with a fraction of their experience and nous, will happily tell you how high the market will be next month and next year, or whether your share will be up or down. Ignore these people. They are paid to have a view, but haven't got a clue. By the way, as an investor who has wasted time in the past trying to predict short-term market/share moves, I'm with those who say it cannot be predicted over this timespan. We can, however, predict that buying good companies with durable economic franchises, sound finances and honest and competent managers at reasonable prices will lead to a good outcome over a span of years – concentrate on finding these companies; don't speculate over market movements.

- Because a share has shown a sequence of up movements (or down movements), this does not give you a clue as to future movements in the same direction. This is the reverse of the gambler's fallacy in which you might believe that fate has determined a bias to future moves that will continue – you might start to believe that, say, down movements are 'representative' of that share and not allow sufficiently for trends to reverse. This is a common psychological block that experiments have shown we humans have.

- Trade frequently. Research has shown that share buyers exhibit a tendency to over-confidence in their ability to quickly analyse dozens of companies, their market environments and the economy. They then act on their latest conclusion resulting in frequent fiddling with their portfolios. The performance of thousands of shareholder portfolios was examined in a large study. They were split into five groups depending on the amount of trading in a year. The idea was that those in the top group, who traded very frequently, resulting in shares flying into and out of their portfolios, were responding to the over-confident side of their psychology. Before costs of trading were taken into account, the share returns were roughly the same for all five groups; doing numerous trades did not add to pre-trading-cost performance. However, after trading costs the best performers were those who traded very little in a year. Warren Buffett says that investors should be issued with a punch card at the start of their investment careers with 20 spaces to punch a hole. Every time you make an investment decision to buy a hole is punched. You only get 20 for a whole lifetime. He is exaggerating to make a point, but you will make far better investment decisions if you do not make too many of them.

- Pull the flowers and water the weeds. Some investors are too quick to sell shares that have risen significantly ('flowers' according to Peter Lynch). 'You can't be wrong taking a profit!' they say. Well, you can, actually. Many companies have the potential of becoming 10 baggers (rising 10-fold), so why would you sell when they have risen a mere 50%. Everything depends on a realistic analysis of future prospects, not an automatic selling off if a good gain is made.

- Another nasty tendency is to hold onto shares that have fallen ('weeds'). It becomes psychologically important to 'at least break even'. How can you tell your spouse that you made a loss? Better to wait awhile until it bounces back. This attitude has cost many investors a fortune over the years. If you can break through this psychological barrier and analyse the business and its management for future prospects, and then sell those that have poor prospects regardless of whether you are already down then you will do much better over the years.

10

Assessing a company

I like to buy things I can understand.

Warren Buffett

Investors versus speculators

People who buy shares without doing the proper analysis under the four headings which follow cannot be termed 'investors'. They are *speculators*. These people do not analyse, they aim for unrealistically high returns and do not build in a margin of safety. Their primary concern is guessing where the market is going to move, not how the underlying business is going to perform. This book is not written for aspiring speculators; there are plenty of books that will tell you how to get rich three times before breakfast already!

This chapter introduces you to some tools to carry out industry analysis and competitive resource analysis. Because this book is a short introduction to investing, I cannot go into much detail on these *corporate strategic analysis* issues. If you would like more consult *The Financial Times Guide to Value Investing* (FT Prentice Hall, 2009) or join us for a day's seminar on the subject.*

This chapter also looks at some of the characteristics of competent and honest managers. Many of these ideas are taken

---

* See *www.glen-arnold-investments.co.uk*

from the writings of great investors. Chapters 11 and 12 provide tools for examining the numbers produced by your company, including whether it has high debt levels, etc. However, there are four fundamental aspects to consider before you buy shares in a company.

The strength of the economic franchise

What we are looking for here is the ability to consistently, over the foreseeable future, generate a high rate of return on the assets that the business uses, i.e. are the profits high relative to the amount of money (in assets) the managers have at their disposal? There are two elements to this:

1 **The competitive structure of the industry**. Do firms in this industry generally generate high rates of return on the capital (assets) that they employ? Or do they, year after year, show losses or returns of less than 5% per year? You might be surprised at just how many industries produce such low rates of return decade in, decade out. As a rule of thumb around 10% is OK, but 20% is excellent.

2 **The competitive position of the firm within the industry**. Does it produce superior profits relative to its rivals? What causes that? What are its *extraordinary resources* allowing it to rise above its rivals? Can it sustain it years into the future?

The quality of the management

Here we are concerned not just with competence, but also qualities such as decency, honesty and integrity. Your managers must show energy, ability and integrity. You need all three. If you have the first two without the third it will kill your investment.

Financial strength

Here we are concerned with questions such as the following.

- Can earnings be increased while utilising little additional capital? It does not serve the investor well if, in order to grow profits, vast amounts of additional money are needed in the business. This will reduce payouts to shareholders to zero.

- If the company went through hard times, would it be able to pay its way or is it vulnerable to upsetting creditors, i.e. is there a large margin of safety on the issue of *solvency*. Does it have low amounts of debt relative to the money put into the business by the equity holders? Are the repayment dates for the debt spread out over a number of future years? Does it have plenty of assets that can be turned into cash at fairly short notice?

- Does it have excellent awareness of the costs of producing its products/services? Many management teams have poor systems for identifying costs.

A low price relative to these qualities

The fact is that you will find dozens if not hundreds of companies that score well on all the points above. **But**, 99% of the time you shouldn't buy – at least not if you are a true investor – because the current market price already fully reflects all these good things; it is at the top end, or over the top end, of a realistic valuation.

Indeed, much of the time good companies are lousy investments because everyone sees them as good companies and the share price more than reflects their enthusiasm.

You must buy only when there is a large *margin of safety*. This means that the range of values you estimate as appropriate for the company is significantly greater than the current market price. This occurs often enough for investors to out-perform the market – if they are patient – but you will not find it happening every week or even every month. The market is generally quite efficient at pricing in the prospects for firms and so you need to be alert for those few occasions when it makes a mistake.

Assessing an industry

In a perfectly competitive industry structure, where outside firms can enter the industry at will, companies can only achieve a *'normal' rate of return*. That is, shareholders receive a rate of return that only just induces them to put money into the firm and hold it there.

The rate of return cannot rise above the normal level to give a supernormal return. Imagine if a perfectly competitive industry did give a very high rate of return temporarily because of, say, a rise in the price of the product. New entrants to the industry, or additional investment by existing competitors, would quickly result in any supernormal return being competed away to take the industry back to the point where the return available is merely that appropriate for the risk level.

Obviously, a perfectly competitive industry is not attractive for investors. Investors need to search for an industry displaying a wide gap between the price of the product and its cost – one producing a high rate of return on the capital taken from shareholders and used by managers. The problem is that competitive forces within many industries continually narrow the gap between price and cost – to push it towards the *competitive floor* – and thus put downward pressure on the rate of return on invested capital.

However, there are some industries in which the competitive forces are weak, permitting supernormal returns to persist over a long period. As an investor you need to search out those industries in which the average firm has a high degree of durable pricing power.

The five competitive forces

Michael Porter produced a framework for analysing the forces driving returns to the perfectly competitive level (Figure 10.1). It goes way beyond simply analysing the degree of rivalry between existing competitors and the potential for entry of new competitors. He pointed out that customers, suppliers and substitutes are also 'competitors' to the firms in an industry in the sense that they impose constraints on the firms achieving supernormal returns.

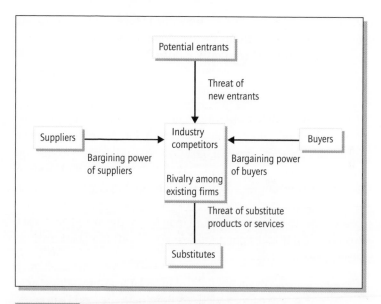

Figure 10.1 The five forces driving industry competition

Source: Adapted from Porter, M.E., *Competitive Strategy: Techniques for Analyzing Industries and Competitors* (Free Press, 2004)

Heinz has few direct competitors because its brand sets it apart and it has an unrivalled distribution system. It faces little threat from the entry of new competitors because the new entrant would need decades to build the necessary brand image and distribution capability. However, Heinz's management is worried because of the increasing power of its customers, the major supermarket chains. The giant food retailers are in a position to ask for a bigger share of the value generated by the sale of the product – to put it more crudely, they can hammer Heinz on price.

The music distribution industry (record producers and retailers) chief executives are scared. It is not that particularly strong current competitors are taking greater market share. This is happening, but it is not the main cause of sleepless nights. Nor are they worried about the entry of new record labels and retail chains. These have come and gone before, and industry returns have remained high. No, their nightmare comes from the internet which allows consumers to download music by file-swapping for virtually nothing. Thus a *substitute* distribution system is a competitive threat to the entire industry.

Steel

The five forces determine the industry structure, which in turn determines the long-run rate of return for the industry. Some industries have an appalling position *vis-à-vis* the five forces and thus make very poor returns. Take steel production in western Europe, for example. Here are some of the largest and most efficient plants in the world. As things stand, the steel firms could hire the best team of managers in the world, but they would still not make good rates of return. All the five forces are against them.

The suppliers of raw materials tend to be large groups with strong bargaining power (three producers dominate the world's iron-ore business, for instance). Many of their customers are enormous groups (particularly the big six car makers who are quite prepared to switch steel supplier unless the keenest prices are offered). There are dozens of low-cost new entrants in Asia and eastern Europe eager to take market share. Within western Europe there is intense rivalry between the existing players because of the need for each participant to produce at a high volume due to the necessity of spreading high fixed costs. This is exacerbated by the difficulty of achieving *exit* from the industry: many companies are seen as national champions and important employers; they thus receive more than just a sympathetic ear from government. On top of all of this there is continual threat of substitutes – for example, the aluminium producers are a constant worry.

Airlines

An industry that has proven to be even worse than steel is airlines. It is astonishing to discover that, after years of management initiatives, cost-cutting, mergers, massive marketing campaigns and all the rest, the cumulative earnings of the industry over its entire history are negative. The fact that passenger numbers grow at a rate other industries would die for (4–5% per year) seems to count for nothing in terms of profitability.

Suppliers are often powerful (e.g. pilot unions). Also, if an airline establishes a profitable market segment it is quickly swamped by new entrants, and by existing airlines moving planes from one part of the globe to another. Over-capacity and low prices are the result. Airlines find it difficult to shed capacity in a hurry; they buy aircraft that fly for decades. When passenger demand falls they simply cannot reduce the supply of aircraft. Exit from the industry is also inhibited by national pride, which leads to suspension of normal commercial logic which might allow unprofitable companies to die.

Threat of entry

If an industry is generating a return above that available in other industries (of comparable risk) it acts as a honey pot – a swarm of hungry insects will try to enter to take away some of the honey. New entrants add to the capacity of the industry as they make a grab for market share. The result is falling prices for every firm in the industry, or the costs of the original industry players rise as they try to maintain sales by spending on marketing, favourable credit terms for customers, and so on.

New entry is definitely something that the incumbent firms abhor. There are two things that can stop, or at least slow down, the advance to the honey pot. First, there could be *barriers to entry* put in the path of the outsiders. Second, a clear message could go out to the aspiring entrants that if they did dare to cross the threshold then they would be subject to a massive retaliatory attack until they were driven out again. Of course, in many industries these two disincentives work in tandem. Examples of industries with strong retaliatory threats include PC software and soft drinks. Try taking on the might of Microsoft or Coca Cola to find out just how high the barriers to entry are.

To overcome established brands such as Mars, Coca-Cola or Nike would cost a vast amount in marketing expense. It would be very expensive for organisations to switch from using Microsoft's operating system and the Office suite. Any potential entrant would need to offer something very special to encourage a switch. Merely offering slightly better performance and a slightly lower price is not good enough.

Substitutes and buyer power

The threat from substitutes dampens profit potential. For example, book retailers' margins are under threat because the internet has provided a substitute method of obtaining books. Buyer power gives customers the potential to squeeze industry margins by forcing down prices, or pressing for higher quality or more services. Tesco has achieved a great deal of buyer power. It is able to exert huge pressure on the firms in the industries producing food, clothes and electrical items.

If the quality of the product is crucial to buyers' systems of operations then they are likely to pay less attention to fine-tuning the price. For example, equipment that is used to prevent oil-rig blow-outs is so vital and costs such a small amount compared with the costs of a blow-out that buyers are willing to pay a little extra to be absolutely sure of complete safety. Similar logic applies to medical equipment. If quality is less important, buyers will be more price-sensitive and shop around among suppliers.

Supplier power

Powerful suppliers are able to set prices that are much greater than their production costs; they are able to appropriate a substantial proportion of the value created in the industries they serve. Suppliers exercise their power by raising prices or reducing the quality of purchased goods and services.

Intel is a powerful supplier to the PC assemblers. Sports rights holders, e.g. English Premier League, and hit TV show producers are powerful suppliers to the TV networks. Coca-Cola sells to an industry (retailers) that is highly fragmented. Most of these buyers have very little power. A few of the large supermarket groups try to exert some authority, but they are up against a powerful brand

and a company used to deciding terms. Coke has over 50% of the carbonated soft drinks market worldwide.

Competitive resource analysis

You need to seek out companies that are strong within an industry with good rates of return. To beat the averages, companies need something special. That something special comes from the bundle of resources that the firm possesses.

Most of the resources are ordinary. That is, they give the firm competitive parity. However, the firm may be able to exploit one or two extraordinary resources – those that give a competitive edge. An *extraordinary resource* is one which, when combined with other (ordinary) resources, enables the firm to outperform competitors and create new value-generating opportunities. It is the ability to generate value for customers that is crucial for superior returns.

Ordinary resources provide a threshold competence. They are vital to ensure a company's survival. The problem is that mere competitive parity does not produce the returns looked for by true investors.

Many successful companies have stopped seeing themselves as bundles of product lines and businesses. Instead, they look at the firm as a collection of resources. This helps to explain the logic behind some companies going into apparently unconnected product areas. The connection is the exploitation of extraordinary resources.

Honda has many different product areas: motor boat engines, automobiles, motorcycles, lawn mowers and electric generators. These are sold through different distribution channels in completely different ways to different customers. The common root for all these products is Honda's extraordinary resource, which is a superior ability to produce engines.

Likewise, photocopiers, cameras and image scanners are completely different product sectors and sold in different ways. Yet they are all made by Canon, which has extraordinary capabilities and knowledge of optics, imaging and microprocessor controls.

The TRRACK system

As an investor, you should not be looking for a long list of extraordinary resources in any one firm. It is great if you can find one – it only takes one to leap ahead of competitors and produce supernormal returns. If two are found, then that is excellent. It is very unusual to come across a company that has three or more extraordinary resources. Coca-Cola is an exception with an extraordinary brand, an extensive distribution system with its connected relationships, and highly knowledgeable managers (knowledgeable principally about how to work the systems in countries around the world to keep the competition authorities off their backs while they tighten control over distribution and prices – allegedly).

To assist the thorough analysis of a company's extraordinary resource I developed the TRRACK system. This classifies extraordinary resources into six categories:

T   Tangible

R   Relationships

R   Reputation

A   Attitude

C   Capabilities

K   Knowledge

Tangible

Occasionally, physical resources provide a sustainable competitive advantage, e.g. McDonald's makes sure that it takes the best locations on the busiest highways, rather than settling for obscure secondary roads; pharmaceutical companies own valuable patents giving some protection against rivalry; even Bugs Bunny might be regarded as a 'physical resource'.

Relationships

Over time, companies can form valuable relationships with individuals and organisations that are difficult or impossible for a potential competitor to emulate. Relationships in business can be of many kinds. The least important are the contractual ones. The most important are informal or implicit. These relationships are usually based on a trust that has grown over many years.

South African Breweries (now SAB Miller) has 98% of the beer market in South Africa. It has kept out foreign and domestic competitors because of its special relationships with suppliers and customers. It is highly profitable. Most of South Africa's roads are poor and electricity supplies are intermittent. To distribute its beer it has formed some strong relationships. It helps truck drivers, many of whom are former employees, to set up small trucking businesses. *Shebeens* sell most of the beer. These are unlicensed pubs. Often they are tiny – no more than a few benches. SAB cannot sell directly to the illegal shebeens. Instead, it maintains an informal relationship via a system of wholesalers. SAB makes sure that distributors have refrigerators and, if necessary, generators. An entrant would have to develop its own special relationship with truck drivers, wholesalers and retailers. In all likelihood, it would have to establish a completely separate and parallel system of distribution. Even then, it would lack the legitimacy that comes with a long-standing relationship.

Reputation

Reputations are normally made over a long period. Once a good reputation is established it can be a source of very high returns. The taste of soup in a can is only learnt by the consumer after purchase. However, it does not take long to learn about the quality of Campbell's soup. Once learned, there tends to be some degree of inertia, leading to consumers being reluctant to switch brands – giving some pricing power.

With car hire in a foreign country the consumer is unable to assess quality in advance. Hertz provide certification for local traders under a franchise arrangement. These local car hirers would see no benefit to providing an above average service without the certification of Hertz because they would not be able to charge a premium price. It is surprising how much more consumers are willing to pay for the assurance of reliable and efficient car hire when they travel abroad, compared with the hiring of a car from an unfranchised local.

Branding is designed to represent and enhance reputations. Brands generally provide a degree of quality certification for consumers. The brand provides the assurance of *consistency*. People buy branded beer because they expect that the next can will taste the same as the ones they bought previously. In many product areas, consumers are reluctant to take the risk of buying unbranded products, for fear of inconsistency of quality (e.g. hamburgers, breakfast cereals and shampoo). The promise of consistency provides a company with a competitive advantage, but the price premium that can be charged for this factor alone is limited because the consistency can be replicated by competitors.

Also required is *incumbency*. Once a brand is established in the minds of consumers it is very difficult for a rival manufacturer to successfully introduce an alternative product, even if that product offers better value. A rival to Cadbury's Flake may offer a chocolate bar of equivalent quality at a lower price, but few consumers will switch – at least not without a vast marketing spend and a long period of time.

Similarly, consumers are attached to ketchup brands and cleaning product brands. Consumer recognition and acceptance of a new product in the face of a well-established incumbent is extraordinarily difficult. The combination of consistency and incumbency can lead to very high returns.

Consumers often use branded products to send *signals* to other people. Nike, Reebok, Levi's exploit this element of human nature and receive a premium price. Signals of high status are generally expensive – Rolls-Royce, Moët et Chandon and Burberry.

Attitude

Attitude refers to the mentality of the organisation. Terms such as 'disposition', 'will' and 'culture' are closely connected with attitude. Every sports coach is aware of the importance of attitude. The team may consist of players with the best technique in the business or with a superb knowledge of the game; they may be the fastest and the most skilful; but, without a winning attitude, they will not succeed. There must be a will to win.

Some firms develop a winning mentality based on a culture of innovation. Others are determinedly orientated towards customer satisfaction, while some are quality-driven. 3M has a pervasive attitude of 'having a go'. Testing out wild ideas is encouraged. Employees are given time to follow up a dreamed-up innovation, and they are not criticised for failing. Innovations such as Post-it notes have flowed from this attitude.

Capabilities

Capabilities are derived from the company's ability to undertake a *set* of tasks. The term 'skill' can be used to refer to a narrow activity or single task. The word 'capability' is used for the combination of a number of skills. Sony developed a capability in miniaturisation. This enabled it to produce a string of products from the Walkman to the PlayStation. It grew by continually reinforcing the various skills needed for technology-based product innovation. This was complemented by marketing flair and strong brands.

In the 1940s, Caterpillar developed a capability for building roads, airstrips and army bases for the US Department of War. It had to develop a wide range of skills as the military needed one supplier that would take on entire projects. Caterpillar offered a worldwide service and supply network for construction equipment at low cost. Having met the challenge set by the military, Caterpillar was in an excellent position after the war to offer a capability rivals could not emulate. It became the dominant firm in the heavy construction equipment industry. Its ability to deliver any Caterpillar part to any location in the world in less than two days was an unbeatable offer.

Knowledge

The retention, exploitation and sharing of knowledge can be extremely important in the achievement and maintenance of competitive advantage. Nike was started by Phil Knight in 1964. He had a special knowledge of the needs of runners – in the 1950s he had been a middle-distance runner in the University of Oregon's track team. He felt that runners had been badly served by the existing manufacturers. He designed shoes using his special insight, but had no special knowledge of manufacturing, and so this was contracted to Asian suppliers. In the 1980s, the company grew from the specialist sports shoe market to the fashion-conscious teenage and youth market. This required an additional set of knowledge attributes: about its customers, marketing and distributors.

Quality of management

You need to search for answers to some key questions about the managers. This may be achieved by, say, meeting them at annual general meetings, observing them over many years, or by questioning people with some familiarity of the company, e.g. customers, suppliers, competitors, employees.

- Are they efficient at handling day-to-day business tasks? Is there a search for continuous improvement? Do they have the courage to try out new ideas?
- Do they plan well ahead of time to keep ahead of the competition? Do they constantly challenge what is now being done?
- Are managers owner-oriented? Will they willingly sacrifice short-term profits to create high shareholder wealth over the long run?
- Do they love the game and like to excel? Are they passionate about their work? Do they relish the thrill of out-performance?
- Are dividends levels high enough so that the managers are

not hoarding cash beyond that needed for shareholder wealth enhancing projects?

- Are they honest about their failures and setbacks?
- Are employees treated decently, with dignity and consideration?
- Are promotions based on merit and not factionalism?
- Does the management team have depth and breadth? Many vivid spirits up and down the management chain?
- Are they constantly bearing down on costs?
- Are they realistic in defining their area of special competence? Do they act decisively on all matters within it? Perform the ordinary extraordinarily well? Ignore even the most enticing propositions falling outside their area of special competence? Persist in diversifying outside their areas of expertise?
- Are they penny pinchers in the executive suite?
- Do they eschew accounting gimmickry?

Profits and balance sheets

You have to know accounting. It's the language of practical business life. It was a very useful thing to deliver to civilization.

Charlie Munger

There are more fun ways of spending time than reading a set of accounts (and the report that goes with them), but it is a necessary task for an investor. They are a primary source of information helping you analyse a company. So this is a topic you are going to have to get to grips with at some point.

The key elements of accounting are simple and it's not necessary for you to deal with the more complex and obscure accounting issues in order to understand the profit performance of a business or the value of the firm's assets. In this chapter, I'll illustrate the essentials of accounting and annual reports using a simple example of a chain of corner shops.

You will then be equipped to read most company accounts straight off. Even if, when examining a firm's accounts, there are things you still do not understand, at least you will be able to ask intelligent questions.

The future is the focus, the past gives us clues

Accounts are backward looking: so why do we bother to look at them? Historical facts about the company are not interesting in and of themselves. They are used to provide clues to what will happen. Directors' performance in using resources in the past (their *stewardship* role) may help assess the likelihood of good managerial performance in the future. The level of debt relative to the amount of the equity capital in the business may provide a clue on the forward risk of bankruptcy. The analysis of past cash flow will help us assess the extent to which future revenues are likely to be swallowed up by investment in plant and machinery rather than being available for distribution to shareholders.

Profit and loss account

The profit and loss account (also called an *income statement*) records whether the company's sales revenue was greater than its costs. It allows you to compare the latest profit with previous years' profits, or with other companies.

Figure 11.1 shows the profit and loss account for our corner shop business last year. Alongside are the income and expenses for the previous year to allow comparison.

The layout and terminology may change from one company to another, but the illustration captures the key figures you are likely to come across. The 'Notes' column points out where in the notes to the accounts to look for more detailed information about a particular item – laid out later in the annual report. Brackets are placed around negative numbers.

The accounts of quoted companies with subsidiaries are described as consolidated. This means that all the income, costs, assets and liabilities of all group companies, whether *wholly owned* or *partially owned*, are brought together in the group's consolidated accounts – see Chapter 2 for a discussion.

	Notes	20x2 £m	20x1 £m
Turnover (revenue)	1	460	400
Cost of sales	2	(280)	(240)
Gross profit	3	180	160
Distribution costs	4	(30)	(22)
Administrative costs	5	(20)	(18)
Other costs	6	(20)	(20)
Operating profit		110	100
Less interest payable ('Finance costs')	7	(12)	(10)
Profit on ordinary activities before tax		98	90
Less tax on profits	8	(28)	(26)
Profit after tax		70	64
Attributable to:			
Equity shareholders of the Company	9	68	62
Non-controlling interests (minority interests)	10	2	2
		70	64
Earnings per share	11	136p	124p
Dividends	12	£34m	£30m
Dividends per share		68p	60p
Retained profit for the year		£34m	£32m

Figure 11.1 Corner Shops plc consolidated profit and loss account for year ended 20x2

Each of the entries in Figure 11.1 will be explained in turn:

Turnover

This is money received or to be received by the company from the sale of goods or services during the year. Other terms used are *revenue* and *sales*. Accounting standards require that profit and loss accounts separate the turnover of continuing operations from activities discontinued during the year and from joint ventures (businesses operated in partnership with other companies).

The notes to the accounts will usually give a more detailed breakdown of where sales came from. For example, Tesco separates turnover into UK, rest of Europe, Asia and 'other'.

For Corner Shops: turnover has risen by an apparently healthy 15%, but you would like to know what proportion of that rise was achieved by the existing operations, by new companies acquired in the year, or by *organic* (that is, non-acquisition) capital growth. (For example, did the company borrow a massive amount to open up 100 more shop branches, leading to sales growth? If so, you may be less impressed by a mere 15% rise.) You might also want to take inflation into account when examining change over time.

Cost of sales

The expense incurred for bought-in raw materials or components, and the costs of bringing materials to saleable condition (including costs of production such as factory wages and manufacturing overheads – obviously not so applicable to Corner Shops).

Gross profit

Turnover less cost of sales.

Distribution costs, administration expenses and other costs

This covers a lot of items, from the expense of employees in head office to the rent paid for a building. *Depreciation* of plant, machinery and other capital items will be included in this section. Depreciation represents the reduction in the stated carrying value of fixed (non-current) assets in the balance sheet.

Operating profit

Also known as *operating income* or *profit from operations*, this is the income remaining after paying all costs other than interest. This may be split between continuing and discontinued operations.

At this point, many accounts show an adjustment for *exceptional items*. These are gains or costs which are part of the company's ordinary activities but are either unusual in themselves or have an exceptionally large impact on profits that year. These one-off items may distort profits in a particular year, so accounts often show results both before and after exceptional items. Examples might include the windfall profits on the sale of an office block, the redundancy costs of closing a subsidiary.

Profit on ordinary activities before tax

Interest paid (and other financing costs) is deducted, or interest received is added, to arrive at the key profit figure: the one that often receives a lot of attention in the press. This is also referred to as the *pre-tax profit* or *pre-tax earnings*.

In the case of Corner Shops net interest paid has risen from £10m to £12m between 20x1 and 20x2. Perhaps interest rates rose and/or the amount borrowed increased in 20x2.

The notes to the accounts will show a breakdown of borrowings – for example, it will lay out the proportion that is repayable within one year, five years, etc.; the amounts borrowed in different currencies; and the amounts borrowed through various bond issues or bank loans.

An analyst might notice that while the turnover has risen by 15%, costs have grown by a larger percentage, so that pre-tax profit rose by only 9% from £90m to £98m.

Taxation

Corporation tax is payable by UK resident companies on all income and capital gains after all costs. The Chancellor of the Exchequer keeps changing the rate of corporation tax, so for illustration we'll stick with 28%.

Note, however, that Corner Shops is not due to pay exactly 28% of £98m (which is £27.44m) in tax. The exact proportion of reported profit paid in tax depends on a number of factors, such as whether tax was paid abroad on income earned abroad. Some companies can pay a very low tax relative to current year earnings because they have tax losses due to trading and other losses made in previous years. When they move into profit they may not have to pay tax for many years. The notes to the accounts should provide details on the computation of tax.

Profit after tax (profit for the period)

This is also called *net profit*. If there are no minority interests then we can call this the *equity earnings* of the company, which belong to the shareholders. However, in the case of Corner Shops one or more of the company's subsidiaries is partly owned by someone else. It is therefore necessary to deduct their slice of the profits.

This is shown by the £2m non-controlling (minority) interest figure. The subsidiary that is only partially owned by our large firm has all its revenues and costs included in the figures presented in the upper half of the profit and loss accounts, and it is only at this point in the accounts that we acknowledge that a proportion of the profits actually belong to outsiders.

So, after deducting minority interests (and possibly dividends on preference shares) the profit attributable to the shareholders in 20x2 is £68m. This is often called the *'bottom line' figure*. When the dividends paid figure is deducted we are left with the funds which have been ploughed back into the business – the *retained earnings* (or retentions).

Earnings per share

This is the profit attributable to ordinary (equity) shareholders (i.e. after non-controlling interests and preference dividends) divided by the number of ordinary shares in issue. The company has issued 50 million shares and so we have earnings per share of £68m/50m = 136p.

Earnings per share is a key measure of a company's performance, allowing investors to observe the growth in profits for each share held. It is easy for management to raise total profits if they keep issuing more shares and thereby bring more money into the business; it is not so easy to raise the earnings on each existing share.

Earnings per share is also a measure of the company's ability to pay dividends in a sustainable manner.

Dividends per share

The total amount paid or due to be paid in dividends for the year (interim and final dividend) divided by the number of shares in issue. For 20x2 this is £34m/50m = 68p per share.

Balance sheet

The balance sheet provides a snapshot of what the company owned and is owed on a particular day in the past: usually the last day of the financial year (or last day of the first half of the year). The balance sheet summarises the assets and the liabilities of the business. The difference between the assets and liabilities is *net assets* or *equity*.

In reports and accounts you will often see two balance sheets. The first is for the *parent company* (*holding company*). This company's numerous wholly or partly owned subsidiaries will be represented on the parent company's balance sheet but not in consolidated form, so this is of limited use for financial analysis. The attention of the investor should be directed at the second balance sheet – the consolidated (or group) balance sheet. To explain the terms in a balance sheet we will work through the items shown in Figure 11.2. (Note that assets are shown as positive figures while liabilities are shown in brackets.)

	Notes	20x2 £m	20x1 £m
Non-current (fixed) assets			
Tangible assets	13	164	160
Intangible assets	14	36	40
Investments	15	10	10
		210	210
Current assets			
Inventory (stock)	16	70	40
Trade and other receivables (debtors)	17	120	80
Current asset investments and deposits	18	40	40
Cash at bank and in hand	19	20	20
		250	180
Current liabilities			
Creditors: amount due within one year	20	(124)	(98)
Net current assets		126	82
Total assets less current liabilities		336	292
Creditor amounts due in more than one year	21	(50)	(40)
Provisions for liabilities and charges	22	(28)	(28)
Net assets		258	224
Equity ('Capital and reserves')			
Called-up share capital	23	10	10
Share premium account	24	100	100
Revaluation reserve	25	46	46
Retained earnings	26	92	58
Total attributable to equity shareholders of the Company		248	214
Non-controlling (minority) interests	27	10	10
Total Equity		258	224

Figure 11.2 Corner Shops consolidated balance sheet at year end 31 March 20x2

Non-current assets (fixed assets)

Non-current assets are those that are not held for resale, but for use in the business. They may be displayed under:

- **Tangible assets**. Assets used to earn revenue that have a physical presence, e.g. land, buildings, machinery and vehicles.
- **Intangible assets**. Things you cannot touch, but which have a long life (longer than one year), e.g. copyright and other publishing rights, licences, patents, trademarks, goodwill, etc.
- **Investments** expected to be held for the long term, e.g. shareholdings in other companies (except subsidiary holdings), works of art, and gilts.

Most long-term assets wear out, and so allowance has to be made for this. Tangible and intangible assets are therefore usually recorded at *net book value*,* which is the original cost of the assets, minus the accumulated depreciation for tangibles, or minus amortisation in the case of intangibles, since their acquisition.

Some assets rise in value. If this happens, companies have the possibility of revaluing assets in the balance sheet. As well as being shown in the fixed assets section, this is also shown in the **revaluation reserve**. The revaluation reserve represents the accumulated revaluations of fixed assets. In this way, a company does not credit the fortuitous increase in value of a fixed asset to the profit and loss account, because this would distort the picture of underlying profitability. (The new International Financial Reporting Standards are less fastidious on this point.)

Investments are generally shown at cost, but investments in stock market quoted securities are often shown at market value in the notes to the accounts.

---

* Under International Financial Reporting Standards some assets may be revalued at 'fair value' which is supposed to relate to some sort of current market value.

Current assets

These comprise cash and assets that can be rapidly turned into cash. Inventories of raw materials, partially finished (work in progress) or finished goods are included here as well as the value of *receivables (debtors)* – that is, amounts owed to the business, usually by customers. Investments expected to be sold within the next year are also included under current assets.

Liabilities

Current liabilities are amounts owed that the company expects to have to pay within the next year. Bank loans with less than a year to repayment and overdrafts will be included here, as will outstanding trade payables (creditors): suppliers allowing the firm to pay later for goods supplied. Also corporation tax due but not yet paid.

The difference between current assets and current liabilities is *net current assets* (commonly known as *working capital*). For Corner Shops, on 31 March 20x2 it amounts to £126 million. If we now add on the value of the non-current assets we have the figure of £336 million for the *total assets less current liabilities*.

Net assets

The net assets figure is the total assets minus all the liabilities. Included in liabilities are those creditor amounts due to be paid after more than a year, non-current liabilities (e.g. long-term bank loans or bonds), and *provisions* for liabilities and charges. A provision is an allowance for a liability if you are unable to be precise about either the amount or when it will be paid. Provisions are often included for items such as pension obligations, restructuring costs (e.g. staff retraining or relocation), environmental damage or litigation.

Equity (capital and reserves)

The net assets of the company are owned by the shareholders. However, there are two groups of shareholders that we have to allow for in a consolidated balance sheet. Some of these net assets are attributable to the holders of the minority fraction of the subsidiaries and not to the holding company shareholders. This amount is represented by the figure for non-controlling interests (minority interests).

The remainder is the net assets attributable to the holding company's shareholders. This is termed *equity shareholders' funds*, or *shareholders' funds* for short. For Corner Shops equity shareholders' funds are allocated to four categories:

- The first is called-up share capital (or simply share capital). If we looked up note 23 we will observe two share capital numbers:
  - The authorised share capital is the nominal (par) value of the shares that were created when the company was established, or which were subsequently created (with shareholder approval). The nominal value of each share might be, say, 5p, 10p, 25p, 50p or any amount the original founders decided upon.
  - The issued (or called-up) share capital is the total value of the shares issued (sold or allotted to investors) when expressed at nominal value. It is normal to observe a company having many more shares authorised than have actually been sold (issued).

The notes usually state both the total number of shares, the nominal value of each share and the total nominal value of all the shares. In this case, there are 50 million shares in issue ('called up'), each with a nominal value of 20p at the end of the 20x2 financial year, thus we see a figure of £10m (the total nominal value) shown in the balance sheet.

When shares are sold they rarely sell at nominal value. We saw earlier in the chapter that our example company is now producing earnings per share of 136p and paying a dividend of 68p. Clearly if the company issued more shares they could sell them for more than 20p – I'd be first in the queue with my 20p if I could get an annual dividend of 68p!

- The share premium account records the additional amount (above the nominal value) that shares were sold for.
- The revaluation reserve arises because assets might be revalued, and it would be wrong to put this increase through the income statement as that would artificially inflate profits that year. For example, when property used for production is revalued upwards, this increase goes straight to the revaluation reserve in the balance sheet.
- The retained earnings (also called profit and loss account) entry in the balance sheet represents the accumulated retained profits for all the years of the company's existence. Notice that this figure rose by £34m between 20x1 and 20x2, reflecting the retention of the profits made in 20x2.

Chairman's statement

The law does not require a chairman's statement, but most companies include one. It can be useful because it helps to put the accounting numbers into context. Events might have occurred which have a significant effect on the profit and loss and balance sheet, and it is often the chairman's statement that flags these. For example, a major acquisition may have taken place, together with a rights issue and a rise in borrowing impacting on the accounts. Without the comment from the chairman, it may not be possible to understand why the accounts show dramatic change from one year to the next.

The statement is also a personal comment from the chairman that will attempt to enlighten the shareholders on the general trading environment that the company coped with in the past and is now faced with. It may also break down the overall performance into constituent parts (e.g. by product line, division or geography) and comment on future prospects for these. Major action, such as factory closures or large investments in new technology, may be referred to. Also some comment will be made on the overall corporate strategy.

Chief executive's review

In addition to the chairman's statement (or sometimes instead of one) there is the chief executive's review or operational review. The review will provide more detail on performance, strategy and managerial intentions for each division.

Directors' report and business review

These are required by law, but directors frequently supply much more information and commentary than either statutes or the Stock Exchange require. The business review is either part of the directors' report or cross-referenced to it. The report contains the following:

- a review of activities during the year and discussion of likely future developments;
- important events affecting the company, which have occurred since the year-end;
- details of share buy-backs;
- technical information, e.g. names of directors and their shareholdings, political or charitable contributions made by the company;
- shareholdings of more than 3% (listed companies only);
- a description of research and development activity;
- policies on employment, supplier relationships, risk management and the environment.

The review (which may be called the *operating and financial review*, *OFR*) provides (ideally) an analysis of the development and performance of the business(es) during the year and a considered, balanced and comprehensive assessment of the position of the company at the year-end. This might touch on corporate strategy and will include a discussion of principal risks and uncertainties. Also included is an analysis based on *key performance indicators* (*KPIs*), which are measures the firm uses to assess its progress and efficiency (see Chapter 12 for some of the ratios commonly used).

There will also be a financial review which tries to explain financial performance. For example, what led to the charging of 'exceptional' costs in the profit statement? Why did debt increase? In what way were the results influenced by foreign exchange rate changes? How does the company limit its risk exposure to interest rates, commodities and currencies? Why has the company embarked on so much capital expenditure? The finance director usually writes the financial review.

Auditors' report

The auditors are appointed by the shareholders at the AGM to hold office until the next AGM. It is a legal requirement to appoint auditors (except for very small companies). Their role is to determine whether the company's financial statements are misleading – whether the accounts show a *true and fair view*. It is an offence for directors to give false or misleading information to auditors. Auditors have the right of access to the books and accounts at all times. They can insist on additional information and explanations from managers to try to obtain an understanding of the financial position.

If auditors have doubts about the quality of record-keeping or they detect a discrepancy between the books and the accounts, or the information and explanations they demand are not forthcoming, they will state the difficulty in their report. That is, they qualify their report. Alarm bells should start to ring when an investor reads the accounts have been qualified.

Five-year summary

Usually placed at the back of the report and accounts is a very useful five- or ten-year summary of key financial data. It is here that you can observe the historic pattern of growth in sales, profits, dividends, earnings per share, and a host of other important variables. An erratic pattern may be less attractive than a smooth one. Fast sales and profit growth with zero earnings per share growth will probably indicate large-scale acquisition of companies combined with regular issuance of shares. This is likely to be less attractive than more pedestrian organic sales and profit growth combined with rising earnings per share.

Beware of relying too much on these summary tables without understanding the detail behind them. Distortions over time can arise because of changes in accounting practice policies, or even accounting standards. Another major source of confusion is the inclusion or exclusion of discontinued activities.

Trading statements

Trading statements (trading updates) tend to be issued by a company three months or so before the annual report or the interim report. They are usually very simple, consisting of a few paragraphs providing a brief description of the firm's trading performance since the last formal report. The financial data supplied is very limited (e.g. 'in the 12 weeks to 15 January sales were down 2%') and profit figures are not provided.

Throughout the year, companies are required to make announcements if they have any information that may, when released, have a significant impact on share price, e.g. losing a major contract.

12

Cash flow and key ratios

If past history was all there was to the game, the richest people would be librarians.

Warren Buffett

Cash flow statement

One of the main reasons why companies go into liquidation is that they run out of cash. It is possible for profits to be on a rising trend and yet to see the company going under. The prospect of liquidation is one of the reasons why you need to examine the cash inflows and outflows of the business over the year.

As well as assessing the likelihood of corporate failure, examining cash flow statements is very useful for filling in some of the gaps in the picture of the company's performance and strength.

It helps answer some key questions such as:

■ What proportion of any increase in profit is swallowed up by ever larger investments in fixed assets, trade receivables and inventories needed to maintain earnings growth?

■ Is anything left for dividends?

■ If investment in assets year after year is greater than cash generated by operations, will the directors have to keep asking shareholders for more money or will they borrow more?

■ If borrowings are increasing how does that affect the risk of the ordinary shares?

■ Does the company generate enough cash to pay its interest?

Furthermore, the cash flow statement is much more difficult for managers to manipulate than the profit and loss account and balance sheet because it is a measure of actual cash movements. It identifies where the company gets its money from and what it spent that money on. Figure 12.1 shows a typical cash flow statement for Corner Shops plc (a continuation of Chapter 11).

	Notes	£m	£m
Cash flows from operating activities			
Cash generated from operations	28		50
Interest paid	7		(12)
Tax paid			(26)
Net cash from operating activities			12
Cash flows from investing activities			
Purchase of property, plant and equipment	13	(10)	
Proceeds from the disposal of property, plant and equip.		0	
Proceeds/purchases of investments		0	
Interest received		0	
Dividends received		0	
Net cash from investing activities			(10)
Cash flows from financing activities			
Increase (repayment) of borrowings	20,21	28	
Ordinary dividends paid	12	(30)	
Net cash used in financing activities			(2)
Net increase/(decrease) in cash and cash equivalents			0
Cash and cash equivalents at the beginning of period			20
Cash and cash equivalents at end of period			20

Figure 12.1 Corner Shops plc consolidated cash flow statement, 20x2

The statement is divided into a number of areas.

Cash flows from operating activities

This includes the cash received from the firm's customers in the year (excluding sales made for which cash has not yet been received and sales taxes, e.g. VAT). Cash paid to suppliers, employees, etc., has been deducted.

We need to recognise that the depreciation in the profit and loss is not a cash outflow. It is a figure estimated by an accountant and then deducted as an expense for that year. Cash flowed out when the item of equipment was purchased, not in the year of depreciation. This means that cash flow is boosted relative to profit because depreciation is not deducted. However, as you will see later, Corner Shops will probably have to pay out cash to buy new equipment in the year, so this lowers cash flow.

Other items that also reduce cash flow relative to profit include the accumulation of more inventory (£30m – see balance sheet change between 20x1 and 20x2 in Figure 11.2) and on more money tied up in trade and other receivables (up by £40m).

If net cash from operating activities is negative we might start to worry because the company may not be selling its goods and services for more than they cost or is pumping vast amounts into working capital (money invested in current assets minus current liabilities) to keep up its sales level.

Under the accounting rules, the cash flow from operating activities is broken down into a lot of detail making the cash flow statement much longer than the one shown in Figure 12.1, e.g. rental income is separately identified.

Cash flows from investing activities

This section includes cash used to pay for the acquisition of fixed assets and/or cash generated by the sale of fixed assets. In the case of Corner Shops a net £10m was spent on long-lived assets – vehicles, equipment, buildings, etc. Cash can also be used to purchase subsidiaries or some of the shares in subsidiaries – cash inflow can increase if these assets are sold.

Cash flows from financing activities

The first two sections of the cash flow statement show the amount of cash generated (or absorbed) by the operating business or through investment activities. For Corner Shops, there is an overall surplus of £2m. However, the company also paid dividends during the year, which used up £30m, leaving it short of cash. This gap was filled by borrowing an additional £28m.

Thus, in this year, the company only just generated enough cash to sustain its investment in working capital items (e.g. stock and receivables) and fixed capital items (e.g. plant and equipment).

It did not produce enough cash to also pay a hefty dividend without borrowing more. This may be a concern to you, an investor. You may like to explore the potential of the firm to produce cash that can be handed out to shareholders. To look at it from a different angle: as the company grows its turnover, does it need large lumps of cash to bolster working and fixed capital just to stay in the game?

Note, our example is unusual in showing zero overall cash movement for the year (£20m in cash at the beginning and at the end). Most will show a significant positive or negative cash balance change.

Cash and cash equivalents

Note that *cash* means notes and coins as well as bank deposits repayable on demand less overdrafts. *Cash flow* includes payments by cheque, etc.

Cash equivalents are short-term investments which can very quickly and easily be sold at low cost to be turned into cash. They are very safe investments so there is very little doubt about the ability of the issuer of the financial instrument being unable to pay. So, for example, it is possible to lend to the UK government by purchasing three-month Treasury bills. These promise to pay £100 to the holder, say, 90 days from now.

These are bought and sold among investors during the 90 days. So, someone might hold a Treasury bill and decide to turn this near cash into cash-in-a-bank-account by selling it for, say, £99.60. A few days later the buyer will collect £100 from the UK government (if he/she does not sell to yet another buyer). The difference between £100 and £99.60 provides a small amount of interest. In 2012, the annual rate of interest on Treasury bills was less than 1% per year, i.e. less than one-quarter of 1% for 90 days.

Example of a *profitable* company forced into liquidation

The moral of the story is the importance of cash flow as well as profits

ManPlace plc starts business after the founders put in total equity capital of £2m by buying new shares. It also borrows £3m from the bank on 1 January. It buys £4m of machinery and hires 25 workers.

The machinery is expected to have a useful life of 10 years and is depreciated (an expense) at a rate of £400,000 per year. In the first year the company is profitable – see Figure 12.2.

	£
Sales	10,000,000
Cost of sales	(8,000,000)
Gross profit	2,000,000
Costs	
Labour	(800,000)
Factory and other costs	(600,000)
Depreciation on machine	(400,000)
Operating profit	200,000
Less interest payable	(160,000)
Profit on ordinary activities before taxation	40,000

Figure 12.2 ManPlace plc profit and loss account

Despite reporting a profit, the company runs out of cash and is forced by its bank into liquidation. It ran out of cash because of a number of factors.

- It granted customers the right to pay for goods 60 days after delivery. In the meantime, ManPlace had to pay its raw material suppliers, labour, machinery and distribution costs while production was taking place. Many customers either paid late (after 60 days) or did not pay at all. Thus the company received only £8m during the year, not £10m.

Also another machine was purchased half way through the year for £500,000. The cash flow statement for the year in this simple case looks far worse than the profit and loss account – see Figure 12.3.

	£
Net cash flow from operating activities	
Cash received from customers is £8m, cash flowing out for cost of sales (bought in materials, etc.) labour, factory and other costs is £9.4m	(1,400,000)
Interest paid	(160,000)
Taxation	0
Capital expenditure	(4,500,000)
Cash inflow (outflow) before financing	(6,060,000)
Cash flows from financing activities	
Issue of shares	2,000,000
Increase in debt	3,000,000
Net increase/(decrease) in cash and cash equivalents	(1,060,000)

Figure 12.3 ManPlace plc cash flow statement (brackets indicate an outflow)

This company started the year with zero cash and ended with negative £1,060,000 cash – clearly unsustainable (even if it did manage to limp to the end of the year).

Key ratios and measures

The idea behind this section is to allow you to analyse a company by focusing on those elements that seem particularly important to you. The value of these ratios and other measures is that they help to put into perspective the numbers reported in the profit and loss account, balance sheet and cash flow statements. They often relate one aspect of the accounts (e.g. profits) to another (e.g. the value of all the assets the company is using).

As well as displaying the relationship between pairs of figures and permitting comparison with other companies, they allow an investor to develop a more informed perspective on the firm's performance and financial standing across time. The way in which ratios change over a period of five or 10 years can help to build up a picture of the company's progress or decline.

Price–earnings ratio

The *price–earnings ratio* or *PER* (*P/E ratio*, the *earnings multiple*) compares a company's share price with its latest earnings per share (eps). The eps is the profit attributable to shareholders after tax deduction, as shown in the profit and loss, divided by the number of shares in issue:

$$PER = \frac{\text{current market price of share}}{\text{last year's earnings per share}}$$

So, for example, if Corner Shops has a current market price of £18 for one of its shares and the eps shown in the latest accounts is 136p:

$$PER = \frac{1800p}{136p} = 13.2$$

The profit attributable to the shareholders is £68m (after subtracting £2m for minority interests) and the number of shares in issue is 50 million, giving eps of 136p.

This PER is called the *historical PER* (or *trailing PER*) because it is based on earnings that have already happened. This is the PER that receives most attention in the press. However, quite often investors are interested in knowing how high the share price is in relation to the level of projected earnings for next year. This is the *prospective PER* or *forward PER*:

$$\text{prospective PER} = \frac{\text{current market price of share}}{\text{next year's expected earnings per share}}$$

Be wary of using someone else's prospective PER – after all, they are forecasting future profits, and might not be good at it, even if they work for a fancy-sounding financial institution.

Some analysts prefer to swap the top and bottom of the PER ratio to create the *earnings yield*. This shows the profits attributable to each £1 invested buying a share:

$$\text{earnings yield} = \frac{\text{earnings per share}}{\text{current market price of share}}$$

For Corner Shops, for every £1 spent buying a share last year's company profits are 7.56p:

$$\text{earnings yield} = \frac{136\text{p}}{1800\text{p}} = 7.56\%$$

Companies sometimes report *diluted earnings per share*. This takes into account any additional shares that may be issued in the future under, say, executive share option schemes or convertible preference shares. The word 'diluted' indicates that the earnings are spread over a larger number of shares so the fully diluted eps will be less than the normal eps reported.

The eps figures used by the press are usually '*basic*' *earnings*. These include a deduction from profit of one-off exceptional items, so they present a warts-and-all picture. Companies often like to present the largest eps figure possible and so they highlight the *headline, underlying, adjusted* or *normalised eps*, which excludes one-off costs, exceptional items and goodwill amortisation. These figures are supposed to show the underlying trend, but some companies seem to have a habit of showing large, supposedly one-off, costs every year. The reassuring titles of these earnings figures belie the fact that directors are able to flatter the company's performance by emphasising these numbers – they neatly sidestep some harsh facts, such as major losses in some of the business's operations.

The PER on its own does not tell you whether a share is appropriately valued. It merely tells you the profit growth that investors are generally expecting. This can then be compared with your estimate of growth to judge whether the market is being realistic, over-pessimistic or over-optimistic. Perhaps your judgement will be influenced by the PERs of other companies, such as those in the same sector, or the PER for the market as a whole. The *Financial Times* publishes industry group and market-wide PERs.

Watch out for managers raising profit!

Increased profit is always a good thing, surely? Well, no. Take the case of Dubious Integrity plc. The managers here get increased pay and bonus depending on the size of the business. Dubious Integrity has 20 million shares in issue and made total earnings after tax of £3m last year. So each share earned 15p. These are currently standing in the market on a PER of 12, i.e. £1.80.

It now takes over Victim plc by buying all its shares for £1 each. Dubious Integrity creates another 20 million shares to hand over to the current owners of Victim in return for their shares. Victim produces profits after tax of £1m per year, thus the consolidated company has £4m of profit, and the managers raise their salaries and bonuses accordingly.

But, what has happened to earnings per share? Profits of £4m divided by 40 million shares is 10p per share – eps has fallen from 15p to 10p. If a multiple of 12 is still applied to each share the price will fall to 120p.

Managers are coining it in, while shareholder value is being destroyed. This line of thought helps to explain why many managerial incentive schemes emphasise eps – to try and get some alignment of managerial self-interest with shareholder wealth. They're not perfect either – managers can game play to raise these artificially.

Gross profit margin (or gross margin)

This is sales minus cost of sales, expressed as a percentage of sales:

$$\text{gross profit margin} = \frac{\text{gross profit}}{\text{sales}} \times 100$$

$$= \frac{\text{sales} - \text{cost of sales}}{\text{sales}} \times 100$$

So, for Corner Shops, where sales are £460m in 20x2 (£400m in

20x1), and the cost of sales £280m (£240m in 20x2), the gross profit margins are:

20x2: £180m ÷ £460m = 39.1%

20x1: £160m ÷ £400m = 40%

Gross profit margin can be used to compare the performance of a company with that of its competitors. If it is low, investigate the reason. It may simply be that the company has a mix of products that have a high level of bought-in raw material costs, or it could be that the management is less efficient, or, perhaps, pricing power in the market place is low. Observations of gross profit over time can likewise prompt further investigation.

Operating profit margin (operating margin, trading margin)

This is operating profit as a percentage of sales. The profit figure used here is profit before interest and tax (PBIT) is deducted. It allows for all the expenses of manufacture, distribution, administration, etc., but not for the financing costs or tax.

$$\text{operating profit margin} = \frac{\text{operating profit}}{\text{sales}} \times 100$$

$$= \frac{\text{sales} - \text{all operating expenses}}{\text{sales}} \times 100$$

For Corner Shops:

20x2: $\frac{£110m}{£460m} = 23.9\%$

20x1: $\frac{£100m}{£400m} = 25\%$

If the company has a declining operating profit margin over time and/or relative to its competitors, this may be a sign of serious trouble – cost control or pricing power may be deteriorating. I'm starting to get concerned because Corner Shops has a declining gross margin and a declining operating profit margin.

Pre-tax profit margin (or pre-tax margin)

This is profit after all expenses including interest, expressed as a percentage of sales:

pre-tax profit margin

$$= \frac{\text{profit on ordinary activities before taxation}}{\text{sales}} \times 100$$

For Corner Shops:

20x2: $\frac{£98m}{£460m} = 21.3\%$

20x1: $\frac{£90m}{£400m} = 22.5\%$

Again the profit margin worsens over time.* This piece of information needs to be combined with others to build up a picture of the company. It must be noted that a pre-tax profit margin of over 20% is still high compared with most firms (mind you, this depends on the industry), so perhaps our company is fundamentally sound but has had a minor downturn in fortunes. We are unable to draw conclusions yet, but we are gaining insight as we gather information.

Return on capital employed (ROCE)

The *return on capital employed* (*ROCE*) measures the return (operating profit) per pound invested in assets within the business.

$$\text{ROCE} = \frac{\text{Profit before interest and tax (operating profit)}}{\text{Capital employed}} \times 100$$

There is no hard-and-fast rule to define capital employed. It may be defined as the total of equity shareholders' funds plus all borrowings. If we assume, for the sake of simplicity, all liabilities are borrowings then for Corner Shops in 20x2:

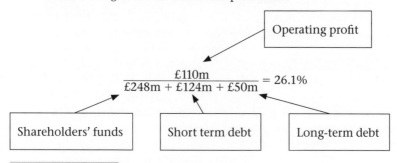

* We would normally observe margin changes over at least five years to avoid drawing conclusions from a period that is too short.

ROCE measures how successful a company is at investing the money it takes from investors (and lenders) in real assets. Corner Shops produces a relatively high ROCE; 26% is likely to be significantly above any cost of borrowing that money or the return that shareholders could get elsewhere for the level of risk associated with holding the shares. If ROCE were less than 8% we would worry, as this is likely to be below the returns achieved by other companies or available elsewhere in the financial markets.

Return on equity (ROE)

It might be interesting to look at the return generated for every pound of *equity capital* – leaving out the return to debt holders and the money put in by lenders, the *return on equity* (*ROE*):

$$\text{ROE} = \frac{\text{profit attributable to shareholders}}{\text{equity shareholders' funds}} \times 100$$

For Corner Shops:

$$\text{ROE} = \frac{£68\text{m}}{£248\text{m}} = 27.4\%$$

This is an impressively high number.

Net asset value (NAV)

Net asset value (*NAV*) (or *book value*) is the total assets of a company minus all liabilities. NAV is often viewed as the break-up value of the company. Should the company be wound up *and* its assets sold at the balance sheet value *and* the liabilities remain as shown on the balance sheet, then the NAV represents the amount available for shareholders after all other claims have been met.

It provides a useful indicator of the value of assets underpinning the shares. However, most shares are rarely valued on NAVs because investors are not looking to liquidate the company, but are anticipating a flow of income from holding shares, and this income flow forms the basis for valuation.

Financial gearing

Financial gearing (or leverage) concerns the proportion of debt in the capital structure. The income you receive as a shareholder can decline more dramatically in a company with high borrowings if there is a small reduction in income. So, for a company with an annual interest bill of £1m and profits (before deduction of interest) of £3m, if profits fall by 50% to £1.5m the income available to shareholders falls from £2m to £0.5m, a 75% decline. On the other hand, if profit before interest rose by 50% to £4.5m, after interest income grows from £2m to £3.5m, a 75% increase. Debt *gears up* profit changes.

A popular gearing measure is the ratio of long-term debt to shareholders' funds (the debt-to-equity ratio).

$$\text{capital gearing (1)} = \frac{\text{long-term debt}}{\text{shareholders' funds}}$$

This may give some indication of the firm's ability to sell assets to repay debts. For example, if the ratio stood at 0.3, or 30%, lenders and shareholders might feel relatively comfortable as there would be, apparently, over three times as much in net assets (i.e. after paying off liabilities) as long-term debt. So, if the worst came to the worst, the company could sell assets to satisfy its long-term lenders. A figure of over 100% would generally be a matter of concern.

A major problem with relying on this measure of gearing is that the book value of assets can be quite different from the saleable value. Also, this measure of gearing can have a range of values from zero to infinity, and this makes inter-firm comparisons difficult. The measure shown below puts gearing within a range of zero–100% as debt is expressed as a fraction of all long-term capital:

$$\text{capital gearing (2)} = \frac{\text{long-term debt}}{\text{long-term debt} + \text{shareholders' funds}}$$

Many firms rely on overdraft facilities and other short-term borrowing. Technically these are classified as short term. In reality, many firms use the overdraft and other short-term borrowing as long-term sources of funds. Furthermore, if we are concerned about the potential for financial distress, then we must recognise that an inability to repay an overdraft can be just as serious as an inability to service a long-term bond. The third capital gearing measure, in addition to allowing for long-term debt, includes short-term borrowing:

$$\text{capital gearing (3)} = \frac{\text{all borrowing}}{\text{all borrowing} + \text{shareholders' funds}}$$

Interest cover and income gearing

It may be wrong to focus exclusively on assets when trying to judge a company's ability to repay debts. A successful advertising agency may not have any saleable assets, apart from a few desks and chairs, and yet it may be able to borrow hundreds of millions because it has the ability to generate cash to make interest payments. Thus, quite often, a more appropriate measure of gearing is one concerned with the level of a firm's income relative to its interest commitments, the *interest cover*:

$$\text{interest cover} = \frac{\text{profit before interest and tax}}{\text{interest charges}}$$

$$\text{or} \quad \frac{\text{operating cash flow}}{\text{interest charges}}$$

The lower the interest cover ratio the greater the chance of interest payment default and liquidation.

If you flip the ratio so that interest charges are on the top you have *income gearing* – measuring the proportion of profits paid out in interest. As a rule of thumb, an interest cover of less than three would be a worry unless the company had exceptionally stable cash flows.

Current ratio

It is useful to know if a company has enough cash and other short-term assets that can fairly quickly be turned into cash to meet its short-term liabilities (does it have *immediate solvency* or *liquidity*?). Can the company pay its near-term bills? The current ratio measures this:

$$\text{current ratio} = \frac{\text{current assets}}{\text{current liabilities}}$$

For Corner Shops:

$$\text{current ratio} = \frac{£250m}{£124m} = 2.02$$

indicating that it has significantly more short-term assets than short-term liabilities – this would be considered prudent (a current ratio less than 1 is cause for worry), but much depends on the nature of the business.

Quick ratio

A large element of the current assets, stock (of raw material, half-finished goods, etc.), may not be easy to quickly convert to cash so a tighter measure of *liquidity* is used, called the *quick ratio, liquid ratio* or *acid test*:

$$\text{quick ratio} = \frac{\text{current assets} - \text{inventory}}{\text{current liabilities}}$$

For Corner Shops:

$$\frac{£250m - £70m}{£124m} = 1.45$$

A quick ratio less than 1 means the company cannot not meet all its current liabilities should they be due immediately. Comparison across an industry is useful for putting the quick ratio figure in perspective, e.g. supermarkets frequently show a quick ratio of around 0.2 – for these firms this is acceptable given that so much of their current assets are rapidly moving stock items matched by high levels of trade creditors (a current liability).

chapter

13

Measuring risk

If you don't risk anything you risk even more.

Erica Jong

I have not hidden from you the fact that investing in shares involves risk. Companies go bust and all shareholder value is lost. There are long periods when individual shares do nothing but follow a downward course, hit by bad news announcements or economic crises. There are also lengthy periods, often more than a decade, when markets as a whole go only one way; that is, down.

Investors cannot avoid risk. We have to take that as given. However, there are sensible actions we can take to reduce risk while not sacrificing overall return. Beyond that we have to accept that there is a trade-off between the size of the return and risk. If you are aiming for very high returns then you have to face very high risk.

Here is an apparently simple question: what is risk? It is far from simple to answer. It has many aspects to it, as you will discover reading this chapter.

The greatest risk of all

The greatest risk of all comes about because share buyers do not understand what they are buying. Frequently, they don't have a clue as to what makes the business tick. We only need go back to the late 1990s to see this tendency as thousands of investors piled into dot-coms despite not being able to assess whether the business model proposed had any hope of success.

The great investors tell us that the best way to reduce risk is to investigate what you are buying into.* Don't flail around buying this, that or the other on a whim, a tip or even broker advice. Find out about the people you are handing your money over to (the directors of the company), about the state of the industry (see Chapter 10), whether the company has any extraordinary resources and the financial standing of the firm (see Chapters 10, 11 and 12).

Risk is proportional to ignorance more than it is proportional to any other factor.

Set against the issue of ignorance of what punters are buying, the technical measures described below are pretty unimportant. Nevertheless, they are referred to by many analysts and journalists, and so you need to know what they are talking about. Later we will look at the measures of risk used by the great investors – you'll find that they are not technical at all, they are qualitative, requiring keen judgement rather than mathematical formulas with Greek letters in them.

Diversification – the nearest thing to a free lunch in investing

We have all heard the adage 'don't put all your eggs in one basket'. This applies to your portfolio as much as to other aspects of life. If you place all your money in one company you are vulnerable to adverse news (e.g. a product failure, chief executive's resignation, government rule change) causing a plummet in price. Holding one company's shares in your portfolio will typically result in volatility.

---

* See Glen Arnold, *The Financial Times Guide to Value Investing*, 2nd edition (Financial Times Prentice Hall, 2009) or join us for a day of seminars on the subject (*www.glen-arnold-investments.co.uk*).

If you split your fund between two companies, at any one time there is a fair chance that bad news affecting one is offset by good news affecting the other, so that overall portfolio returns do not oscillate as much. This principle works even better if you have three, four or five shares in your portfolio

Ice cream and umbrellas

To illustrate the benefits of diversification let us take an extreme example. My aim here is to eliminate all volatility in profits so that year after year the same return comes through to shareholders regardless of the underlying circumstances. Thus there is no bobbing about at all, returns remain perennially good.

Start by imagining that you own an ice cream business in a seaside town. If the summer is hot, profits are very high. If the summer is cold, you lose money – a lot of hard work for no return that year. If the summer is typically British, with a mixture of showers and sun, then you make modest profits. These modest profits are perfectly acceptable as a rate of return on your money invested.

Of course, when you bought this business you had no idea what the weather would be over the next 10 years; just that you have to take the rough with the smooth. Profits from year to year are going to be volatile, but over, say, a decade you will make an acceptable return on the money invested – it will average out OK.

Now I'll demonstrate the benefits of diversification. Instead of putting all your money into the ice cream business you devote half to ice cream and half to the selling of umbrellas. Now what happens? When it is sunny, your ice cream business makes bumper profits, but your umbrella business loses money resulting in an overall average return, acceptable but not brilliant. When it is wet, the umbrella business has a great time of it, but you lose money on the ice creams resulting, again, in acceptable profits overall. When the weather is mixed, both businesses produce acceptable returns.

Thus we have a free lunch: Investing purely in ice cream results in 'an acceptable return', say 10% averaged over a lot of years. So does investing in a portfolio of two businesses: 10% return per year.

However, the portfolio gives you something else: without having to sacrifice any return (over a span of years) you bring volatility down to zero.

The stock market is a little different in that the returns between two companies, say M&S and Rolls-Royce, do not move exactly in opposite directions from one year, or one month, to the next. There is generally a small degree of different movement but not much. Nevertheless this is enough, if the portfolio gets to around 10–15 shares, for the effects of portfolio diversification to be very beneficial. You will not eliminate all volatility but you will reduce it **without** sacrificing overall return†. The typical effects of stock market diversification are illustrated in Figure 13.1.

Diversification is a cheap and practical way of reducing your risk. You are highly recommended to do it. However, note that in Figure 13.1 the benefits of further diversification after a handful of different shares are held in the portfolio tail off – you can keep

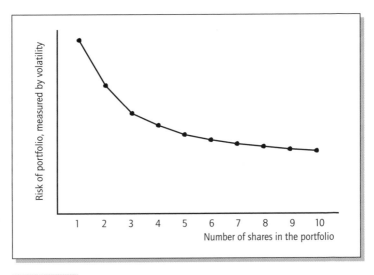

Figure 13.1 Decreasing risk by portfolio diversification

† Remarkably, the benefits of diversification work even when the shares move together in the same direction. This co-movement cannot be 'perfect' though – see below for perfect positive correlation.

on reducing risk, but the additional benefit starts to become very small.

I suggest that private investors should not over-diversify because the benefits of additional diversification become tiny and yet the disadvantage of not being able to understand all the companies you are buying a portion of which starts to loom large. Not only do you sacrifice the ability to understand the companies at the time of share purchase, but you are unable to follow the unfolding stories thereafter if you are trying to keep track of dozens of shares.

Note also that the benefits of diversification are very much reduced if you buy shares all in the same sector of the market (e.g. all telecommunications shares). These are likely to go up and down together.

Volatility

Let's take a closer look at this term 'volatility'. Warning: this is about to get mathematical – you can skip the detail of the calculations without losing much comprehension of the volatility measures.

Figure 13.2 shows the share prices for two companies over a period of eight weeks. It is obvious from the chart that shares in Bouncy plc are much more volatile than shares in Stable plc. The average price for both shares is £1.

Observing the higher degree of movement in Bouncy's shares around its average share price is very easy in this case. However, it might be useful to summarise the degree of movement in a number (a 'statistic'), particularly if we were looking at more subtle cases and could not gauge relative volatility by looking at a chart.

The measure used by many in the financial markets is called *standard deviation.* This is calculated by looking at the difference between the average share price over the entire study period (eight weeks in this case) and the actual share price in each week.

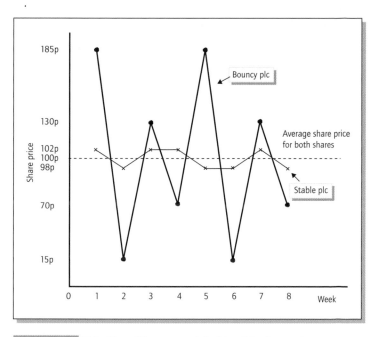

Figure 13.2 Volatility of Bouncy and Stable plc's share prices

In the case of Stable plc the difference is 2p in each week (102p − 100p or 100p − 98p). Each of these differences (deviations) is squared and then the squares are added together:

$$2 \times 2 + 2 \times 2 + 2 \times 2 + 2 \times 2 + 2 \times 2 + 2 \times 2 + 2 \times 2 + 2 \times 2 = 32$$

The number 32 is then divided by the number of occasions; in this case 8 (weeks). This gives us the *variance* of the share price of Stable, 4, over the period of eight weeks and is a measure of risk in its own right.

This is a large number compared with the size of the weekly movements around the average – only 2p. This is because we squared the weekly deviations. So, what we do to bring us back to the same units as the original data is to take the square root of the variance: the square root of 4p is 2p, this is the standard deviation.

If we follow the same procedure for Bouncy:

$85 \times 85 + 85 \times 85 + 30 \times 30 + 30 \times 30 + 85 \times 85 + 85 \times 85 + 30 \times 30 + 30 \times 30 = 32,500$.

Dividing 32,500 by 8 we get 4062.5p, the variance and then, taking the square root, a standard deviation of 63.7p.

So now, instead of having a general impression of Bouncy's higher volatility we have precise measures: Bouncy's standard deviation, at 63.7p, has been many times greater than Stable's, at a mere 2p. High standard deviation is regarded as a bad thing because investors do not like to be caught out with a downswing in the market price. They like the upswing but, given a fixed overall return, would prefer a degree of movement that is closer to the average. They 'feel the pain' of the underperformance more than the joy of the equal-sized out-performances.

In reality, when calculating standard deviation analysts will examine more than eight periods. So they might use three years of monthly data or one year of daily data, for example. Also total return (including dividends as well as price movement) rather than share price could be analysed.

Be aware that, as investors, we are interested in the likelihood of loss in the *future*. Variance and standard deviation tell you about *past* volatility. It is a leap of faith to then assume that the future will be like the past. You need to examine the circumstances to see if such faith can be justified. It is remarkable how measures of standard deviation change over time for the same company; volatility calculated two years ago puts the company into the low-risk category but one calculated last month puts it into the high-risk category.

Correlation

Correlation measures the degree to which the returns of two assets move together. Correlations are described on a scale that stretches from -1 to $+1$.

A perfect positive correlation $(+1)$ means that the two assets move in lock step with one another. So, if Tesco's share price went up or down by a certain percentage and Sainsbury always went up or down by the same percentage then Tesco and Sainsbury would have *perfect positive correlation.* There is no reduction in volatility for a portfolio of perfectly correlated shares – it is merely averaged.

A correlation of −1 is *perfect negative correlation.* This time the movements are exact opposites, as in the case of our umbrella company and ice cream company. If they moved in opposite directions most of the time but not perfectly, then the correlation coefficient could be, say, −0.5. Assets that do not have any co-movement at all – if one goes up the other may either go up or down – show a correlation of 0.

Diversification is going to be most effective with shares that are negatively correlated. You may have noticed that when the London equity market is up the equity markets in the USA and in Europe are also (generally) up. This impression is confirmed by the calculation of correlations which turn out to be around 0.6−0.9.

Beta and alpha

Beta measures the extent to which a share has, historically, gone up when the market as a whole rose, and gone down when the market went down. It is a share's sensitivity to the market movements.

A beta of 1 indicates that generally (on average) in the past when the market rose by 10% this share rose by 10%. A beta of, say, 2 indicates a high sensitivity to market movements in the past. If the market rose by 10% this share tended to rise by 20%. This is fine if things are going well – you outperform the market. On the other hand, if the market fell by 10% your share showed a tendency to exaggerate the market movement by falling 20%.

Shares with betas under 1 have historically been more stable than the market as a whole. So, a share with a beta of 0.5 generally responded to a 10% fall in the market by only falling 5%. The danger of relying on beta for future-orientated investment decisions is that you have to assume that the relationship with market returns will continue. This is often not the case.‡

Alpha is a measure of a performance greater or less than the market as a whole after allowing for beta. It is the portion of a share's return that cannot be explained by its responsiveness to moves in the market as a whole.

Some more types of risk

Liquidity risk

Liquidity is the degree to which an asset can be sold quickly and easily without loss in value. Property investment assets are relatively illiquid investments because they may take weeks to sell. I knew this before 2008, but it really hit home when trying to sell two properties in a market where liquidity almost totally disappeared. If a quick sale is needed, a reduction in price is usually required.

Shares are generally more liquid than property, but they can still be hard to sell quickly and without moving the price against you. If other investors and market makers see you coming with a lot of shares that are infrequently traded they may well drop the price. Smaller company shares tend to be most illiquid. There are medium-sized firms where the majority of shares are held by a family or a few close associates. Trading here can be thin and illiquid. Many stock market listed companies see only one trade per month.

Event risk

September 11, the 2008 crisis and the eurozone crisis were events that had profound impacts on companies. Event risk is the risk of suffering a loss due to unforeseen events. It could be less dramatic than depression or war, e.g. a merger, or a loss of a major contract.

---

‡ For a discussion of the profound difficulties with relying on beta as a measure of risk see Chapter 8 of the fifth edition of Arnold, G. (2013) *Corporate Financial Management*, Pearson Education.

Political risk

Changes in government or government policies may affect investors. This is more usually the case in developing countries where confiscation or forced nationalisation could take away all value from an overseas shareholding. In 2012, the Argentine government simply took an oil company from the Spanish firm Repsol.

Even limits on dividends can have an impact. Note that investors in UK listed companies conducting activities abroad can be affected by political events in other countries.

Exchange rate risk

It is possible to lose money on investments abroad simply because the foreign exchange rate moves against you even if the value of the shares (when valued in the overseas currency) remains constant. However, if you are diversified internationally you may be able to take a swings-and-roundabout attitude to this risk.

Market risk

Your investment could be affected by a general slide in the whole stock market. Shares should not be seen as short-term investments because unexpected downward movements in the markets happen regularly – you must allow time for shares to perform well.

Inflation risk

If you select 'safe' investments such as building society accounts or government bonds you may suffer from inflation risk. That is, what seems like a reasonable return when inflation is 2% loses purchasing power if inflation rises in the future to, say, 10%.

Investors in government securities were very badly hit in the 1970s as inflation rose to over 20%: they had fixed their 'safe' returns at around 5–6%. In 2012, bond investors are accepting a locked-in rate of return of around 2% over 10 years or more. It seems to me that they are taking a big bet on inflation (and therefore interest) rates remaining low.

The safer approach to dealing with inflation risk is to buy shares at reasonable prices relative to their long-term prospects. There have been occasions in financial history when the riskier investments were bonds. I know, this is the opposite of conventional thinking.

Great investors' views on risk

What do the great investors regard as the best measure of risk? Surprisingly, perhaps, they do not use the mathematically based measures so much talked about by those bright young graduates in the markets. They're just old fuddy-duddys with a simplistic homespun view of risk unable to cope with the magnificence of the mathematical models created in recent times! Perhaps.

Or are they really on to something more profound by concentrating on factors which while impossible to measure with great precision are nevertheless more important? Personally, I'd rather be roughly right than precisely wrong so I'll stick with the subjective measures of risk. Apart from anything else, they are focused on losses over the long term rather than over a span of days or weeks (as the mathematical measures are). Investors, by definition, are long-term focused.

Warren Buffett

In our opinion, the real risk that an investor must assess is whether his aggregate after-tax receipts from an investment (including those he receives on sale) will, over his prospective holding period, give him at least as much purchasing power as he had to begin with, plus a modest rate of interest on that initial stake. Though this risk cannot be calculated with engineering precision, it can in some cases be judged with a degree of accuracy that is useful. The primary factors bearing upon this evaluation are:

1 The certainty with which the long-term economic characteristics of the business can be evaluated;

2 The certainty with which management can be evaluated, both as to its ability to realize the full potential of the business and to wisely employ its cash flows;

3 The certainty with which management can be counted on to channel the rewards from the business to the shareholders rather than to itself;

4 The purchase price of the business;

5 The levels of taxation and inflation that will be experienced and that will determine the degree by which an investor's purchasing-power return is reduced from his gross return.

These factors will probably strike many analysts as unbearably fuzzy, since they cannot be extracted from a data base of any kind. But the difficulty of precisely quantifying these matters does not negate their importance nor is it insuperable.

Is it really so difficult to conclude that Coca-Cola and Gillette possess far less business risk over the long-term than, say, *any* computer company or retailer? Worldwide, Coke sells about 44% of all soft drinks, and Gillette has more than a 60% share (in value) of the blade market. Leaving aside chewing gum, in which Wrigley is dominant, I know of no other significant businesses in which the leading company has long enjoyed such global power.

... The might of their brand names, the attributes of their products, and the strength of their distribution systems give them an enormous competitive advantage, setting up a protective moat around their economic castles. The average company, in contrast, does battle daily without any such means of protection.

The competitive strengths of a Coke or Gillette are obvious to even the casual observer of business. Yet the beta of their stocks is similar to that of a great many run-of-the-mill companies who possess little or no competitive advantage. Should we conclude from this similarity that the competitive strength of Coke and Gillette gains them nothing when business risk is being measured? Or should we conclude that the risk in owning a piece of a company – its stock – is somehow divorced from the long-term risk inherent in its business operations? We believe neither conclusion makes sense and that equating beta with investment risk also makes no sense.

Source: Buffett, W. (1993) Letter accompanying the Annual Report for Berkshire Hathaway Inc. for 1993

Benjamin Graham

We should like to point out that the words 'risk' and 'safety' are applied to securities in two different senses, with a resultant confusion in thought.

A bond is clearly proved unsafe when it defaults its interest or principal payments. Similarly, if a preferred stock or even a common stock is bought with the expectation that a given rate of dividend will be continued, then a reduction or passing of the dividend means that it has proved unsafe. It is also true that an investment contains a risk if there is a fair possibility that the holder may have to sell at a time when the price is well below cost.

Nevertheless, the idea of risk is often extended to apply to a possible decline in the price of a security, even though the decline may be of a cyclical and temporary nature and even though the holder is unlikely to be forced to sell at such times.... But we believe that what is here involved is not a true risk in the useful sense of the term. The man who holds a mortgage on a building might have to take a substantial loss if he were forced to sell it at an unfavorable time. That element is not taken into account in judging the safety or risk of ordinary real-estate mortgages, the only criterion being the certainty of punctual payments. In the same way the risk attached to an ordinary commercial business is measured by the chance of its losing money, not by what would happen if the owner were forced to sell ...

... [T]he bona fide investor does not lose money merely because the market price of his holdings declines; hence the fact that a decline may occur does not mean he is running a true risk of loss. If a group of well-selected common-stock investments shows a satisfactory overall return, as measured through a fair number of years, then this group investment has proved to be 'safe'. During that period its market value is bound to fluctuate, and as likely as not it will sell for a while under the buyer's cost. If that fact makes the investment 'risky', it would then have to be called both risky and safe at the same time. This confusion may be avoided if we apply the concept of risk solely to a loss of value which either is realised through actual sale, or is caused by a significant deterioration in the company's position – or more frequently perhaps, is the result of the payment of an excessive price in relation to the intrinsic worth of the security.

Source: Graham, B., *The Intelligent Investor*. Revised 4th edn (Harper Collins, 1973)

14

Companies selling shares to outsiders

A stockbroker urged me to buy a stock that would triple its value every year. I told him, 'At my age, I don't even buy green bananas'.

Claude Pepper

Most of the time you will be buying second-hand shares, but occasionally there is an opportunity to buy newly created shares directly from the company when it makes an issue to the public. When a firm does this by coming to a stock market for the first time it is called a *new issue, a flotation* or, following growing Americanisation, an *initial public offering (IPO)*.

Can be good, but be cautious

Buying shares in IPOs can be a good deal. As well as avoiding brokerage fees and stamp duty tax when buying, you might find that the company and its advisers have deliberately priced the shares a fraction below what they think the market will pay. They are concerned to ensure that the shares get away to a good start, and that the shares go up in the first few days rather than down. They do not want newspaper headlines of 'shares falling due to being overpriced'.

Many great companies started as small companies raising a few million when they first joined the market, e.g. Tesco, eBay and Google. Imagine being a buyer of one of those in the early days! Or being a buyer of LinkedIn shares in 2011 when they rose more than 100% on the first day.

On the other hand, you can lose money on IPOs if you do not properly examine the company and pay a reasonable price rather than the hyped price, e.g. Ocado shares went from the £1.80 it charged new investors in July 2010 to less than £1 a few months later. Facebook was launched at a price of $38 in June 2012; within days it was under $31 and eventually halved. So, caution is required, as well as sound analysis (see Chapters 10–12 for guidance). IPOs are not a guaranteed road to riches.

Strict rules

This chapter not only tells you about the process of bringing a company to market for the first time but, in doing so, highlights the safeguards put in place to minimise the risk of charlatan companies defrauding you. The various finance professionals involved in the process might seem an expensive extravagance, but they help to keep the market (mostly) clean of unsound companies building castles on sand and outright fraudsters determined to sell on a sham business.

Not all IPOs involve new shares

In fact, there are two potential sources of the shares sold in an IPO:

1 The existing shareholders sell a proportion or all of their shares. If you buy, your cash goes to them. Always ask why they are they getting out, if it is such a great company in which to invest.

2 Completely new shares are issued to the new buyers and the money flows to the company to permit it to expand, pay off debt, etc.

Quite often it is a mixture of the two.

The sponsor

The United Kingdom Listing Authority (UKLA) is responsible for approval of the prospectuses and admission of companies to the Official List. It is a division of the main financial markets regulator the Financial Conduct Authority. In addition the London Stock Exchange (LSE) has to admit companies to its Main Market. Thus a floating company has to go through two parallel processes to gain (i) a 'listing' with the UKLA and (ii) admission to trading on the MM.

When the directors decide it is time to float the company they will quickly realise that they lack the expertise needed to bring the project to fruition. They need the help of a number of specialists. The key adviser is the sponsor. This may be an investment bank, stockbroker or other professional adviser (e.g. accountant) approved by the UKLA.

The sponsor (sometimes called the *issuing house*) will discuss with the directors the nature of the business and the aspirations of the management team. They will be probing to see if flotation really is the most suitable route for the company to take. The sponsor usually has a high reputation in the City and will be putting this reputation on the line if it recommends a company to investors – sponsors regularly drop unsuitable companies.

One of the key things the sponsor will examine is the management team. There must be sufficient range and depth, and a high degree of continuity and stability over recent years. Investors do not like to be reliant on the talents of one individual and so will expect an able team. The sponsor may even – quite forcefully – recommend additional directors, supplementing the team to bring it up to the required standard.

The sponsor will also make sure the company complies with the usual rule of having three years of accounting figures. Another key rule is that the company is willing to allow at least 25% of its share capital to be in public hands.

Additional tasks for the sponsor include drawing up a timetable for the flotation, advising on the method of flotation (e.g. placing or offer for sale) and coordinating the activities of a raft of other professional advisers involved in the project.

The prospectus

The most important document in the process is the prospectus. The sponsor helps to draft this alongside the directors (who carry ultimate responsibility for its accuracy). It is designed to reveal a lot of facts about the company to investors. It will probably contain far more information about the firm than it has previously dared to put into the public domain. The UKLA lays down stringent requirements for the content of the prospectus. Even without these, the company has an interest in producing a stylish and informative document as it acts as a marketing tool attracting investors.

When examining a prospectus, bear in mind the following:

- A trading record of three years is the minimum requirement, but you will often be presented with detailed accounts going back five years. Examine these carefully.

- Consider the information given about the growth trajectory of the company. Look at its history, its current position and the, no doubt rosy, picture painted by the directors of its prospects. Do you share their optimism about the industry and about this company's competitive strength within the industry?

- If the company is selling new shares, does it have a sound strategy for spending the money it raises? Or does it sound vague, using phrases such as 'we are raising funds to exploit future business opportunities' or to 'provide working capital'. It could be that the directors are primarily interested in growing the business for themselves (higher status, salaries, etc.) rather than for shareholders and they see a chance of persuading gullible investors to part with their money.

- All businesses face risks. The writing of the prospectus should have forced the directors to think about and list the risks facing the firm. For example, is the firm heavily dependent on one customer? Does it rely too much on overdrafts rather than long-term loans? Does it have too much debt? Are its sales vulnerable to political change in a volatile part of the world? To allow investors to assess these risks, the prospectus will lay out details on types of debt (e.g. repayment at short notice or after two, five and 10 years, bank loans versus bonds, currency of interest and capital payments) and state whether there is sufficient working capital. Also all major contracts entered into in the past two years will be detailed. Analysis of sales by geographic area and category of activity will help you assess the riskiness of the businesses, as will the information on research and development and significant investments in other companies. Statements by experts are usually required: valuers confirm the valuation of property, engineers comment on the viability of processes or machinery, accountants comment on profit figures. As a further safeguard, the prospectus is required to bring to the attention of potential shareholders any risk element apparent to the directors or sponsors that has not already been disclosed.

- Who owns the shares in the company? Is there a dominant shareholder who might exploit his position to reduce returns to smaller shareholders to boost his own? To help you here, the rule is that all persons holding more than 3% have to be named.

- Is the dividend policy acceptable to you? Some companies (e.g. hi-tech firms) have a policy of ploughing back all the money generated (if there is any) and so won't pay dividends for some years.

- Examine the information given on the directors' and senior managers' backgrounds and reward systems. Which other companies have they worked for? Have they set up a number of companies and abandoned them when they faltered? How many were liquidated? How much are they being paid? Are pay and performance linked in a way that means that they do well only if shareholders are doing well? Does the company do business with another company owned by one or more of the directors (e.g. renting a factory owned by a private company associated with a director)?

Finding out about new issues

Each week the *Financial Times* and the *Investors Chronicle* discuss companies that are due to float in the following months. Both these publications display statistics of recent new issues. The website of the LSE (*www.londonstockexchange.com*) carries details on the new issues. Other websites concerned with new issues include Hemscott (*www.hemscott.com*), Interactive Investor (*www.iii. co.uk/newissues*), Proactiveinvestors (*www.proactiveinvestors.co.uk*) and ALLIPO (*www.allipo.com*).

Brokers usually offer a new issues service. You will be sent details of all new issues which your broker is willing to apply for. (Many new issues are only open to large buyers, such as pension funds and insurance companies. However, brokers are allowed to collate small-investor applications and then buy shares in bulk in the same way as an institution.)

Underwriting

The sponsor generally *underwrites* the issue. In return for a fee, underwriters guarantee to buy any shares not taken up by the market. This is a kind of insurance for the company – come what may, it will raise the money it needs to fulfil its strategic objectives.

The sponsor generally charges a fee of 2–4% of the issue proceeds and then pays part of that fee, say, 1.25–3.0%, to *sub-underwriters* (usually large financial institutions) who each agree to buy a certain number of shares if called on to do so. In the vast majority of cases the underwriters do not have to purchase any shares and so walk away with thousands or millions of pounds in fees. However, there are occasional flops when they are forced to buy shares no one else wants, resulting in the shares *overhanging* the market. This problem affected the IPO of Facebook, when the underwriters had to buy a lot of shares.

Attempts have been made by some companies to go below the standard 2–4% cost of underwriting, but the majority continue to accept this as the going rate. It is a 'nice little earner' for the City institutions, and they like to keep it that way.

The role of the corporate broker

Brokers play a vital role in advising on share market conditions and the likely demand from investors for the company's shares. They also represent the company to investors to try to generate interest. When debating issues such as the method to be employed, the marketing strategy, the size of the issue, the timing or the pricing of the shares, the company may value the market knowledge the broker has to offer. Brokers can also organise sub-underwriting, and in the years following the flotation may work with the company to maintain a liquid and properly informed market in its shares. Brokers also help with subsequent share issues, e.g. rights issues (see Chapter 15).

Methods of flotation

The sponsor will look at the motives for wanting a quotation, at the amount of money that is to be raised, at the history and reputation of the firm, and will then advise on the best method of issuing the shares. The final choice often rests on the costs of the method of issue, which can vary considerably. Here are the main options:

- **Offer for sale**. The company sponsor offers shares to the public by inviting subscriptions from institutional and individual investors. Investors will need to contact the sponsor or the broker to obtain an application form and read the propectus. Normally the shares are offered at a *fixed price* determined by the company's directors and their financial advisers.

- **Introduction**. Introductions do not raise any new money for the company. If the company's shares are already quoted on another stock exchange or there is a wide spread of shareholders, with more than 25% of the shares in public hands, the Stock Exchange permits a company to be 'introduced' to the market. This method may allow companies trading on AIM to move up to the Main Market or foreign corporations to gain a London listing. This is the cheapest method of flotation since there are no underwriting costs and relatively small advertising expenditures.

- **Placing**. In a placing, shares are offered to the public but the term 'public' is narrowly defined. Instead of engaging in advertising to the population at large, the sponsor or broker handling the issue sells the shares to a select group of institutions such as pension and insurance funds. The costs of this method are considerably lower than those of an offer for sale. There are lower publicity and legal costs. A drawback of this method is that the spread of shareholders is going to be more limited. To alleviate this problem the Stock Exchange does insist on a large number of placees holding shares after the new issue. As this method is much cheaper and easier than an offer for sale, companies have naturally switched to placings, thus excluding small investors from most new issues.

- **Intermediaries offer**. This method is often combined with a placing. Shares are offered for sale to financial institutions such as stockbrokers. Clients of these intermediaries can then apply to buy shares from them.

- **Book-building**. Selling new issues of shares through book-building is a popular technique in the USA. It is starting to catch on in Europe. Under this method the financial advisers to an issue contact major institutional investors to get from them bids for the shares. The investors' bids are sorted according to price, quantity and other factors such as 'firmness' of bid (e.g. 'we will buy regardless of market conditions'). This information may then be used to establish a price for the issue and the allocation of shares.

- **Reverse takeover**. Sometimes a larger unquoted company makes a deal with a smaller quoted company whereby the smaller company 'takes over' the larger firm by swapping newly created shares in itself for the shares in the unquoted firm currently held by its owners. Because the quoted firm creates and issues more new shares itself than it had to start with, the unquoted firm's shareholders end up with the majority of the shares in the newly merged entity. They therefore now control a quoted company. The only task remaining is to decide on a name for the company – frequently the name of the previously unquoted company is chosen. A reverse takeover is a way for a company to gain a listing/quotation without the hassle of an official new issue.

Underpricing and stagging

The company floating is usually keen to have its offer fully taken up by public investors and so may underprice the shares, giving an opportunity for the buyers. They can buy the shares from the company and then sell immediately following receipt. This is called *stagging*.

Stagging for private investors is rarely possible these days as most new issue shares go to institutions in a placing. However, there are occasional opportunities in intermediaries offers or (rare) offers for sale.

How does an AIM flotation differ from one on the Official List?

The Alternative Investment Market (AIM's) rules are kept as relaxed as possible to encourage a wide variety of companies to join and keep costs of membership and capital raising to a minimum. However, it is felt necessary to have some vetting process for firms wishing to float on the AIM. This policing role was given to *nominated advisers* who are paid a fee by the company to act as unofficial 'sponsors' in investigating and verifying its financial health. When the nominated adviser's fee is added to those of the Stock Exchange, accountants, lawyers, printers and so on, the cost can be as much as 10–40% of the amount being raised.

The AIM was designed so that the cost of joining was in the region of £40,000–50,000. But, this figure has now risen so that frequently more than £500,000 is paid. Most of the additional cost is for raising funds by selling newly created shares rather than just joining AIM, which costs about £100,000–200,000. The nominated advisers argue that they are forced to charge firms higher fees because they incur more investigatory costs due to the emphasis put on their policing role by the Stock Exchange. The cost of joining the Main Market is generally above £500,000, plus the cost of raising money by selling shares.

After flotation

The UKLA insists on listed companies having *continuing obligations*. One of these is to ensure that all price-sensitive information is given to the market as soon as possible and that there is *full and accurate disclosure* (and all investors to receive it at the same time).

Information is price-sensitive if it might influence the share price or the trading in the shares. Investors need to be sure that they are not disadvantaged by market distortions caused by some participants having the benefit of superior information. Public announcements will be required in a number of instances, for example: the development of major new products; the signing of major contracts; details of an acquisition; a sale of large assets; a change in directors; a decision to pay a dividend. The website *www.investegate.co.uk* shows all major announcements made by companies going back many years – as do most (free) financial websites.

15

Seasoned equity offerings

Know what you own, and know why you own it.

Peter Lynch

A seasoned equity offering is a new issue of shares by a company that is already on a public exchange. In many instances these shares are sold to existing shareholders, such as through a rights issue. In other cases outsiders may buy the shares. In this chapter, I explain what you need to look out for when a company is raising money this way.

Rights issues

A rights issue is an invitation to existing shareholders to purchase additional shares in the company. This is a very popular method of raising new funds, and if you hold a portfolio of any size you'll find that you are regularly being asked to stump up more cash for one company or another.

To do a rights issue the directors are usually not required to seek the prior consent of shareholders, and the LSE will only intervene in larger issues (to adjust the timing so that the market does not suffer from too many issues in one period), so it is seen as a relatively straightforward way of raising fresh equity capital.

To inform you properly about the issue of more shares, and entice you to buy some, the company will send you a prospectus. It will explain how the new money will be spent. Perhaps your company sees an opportunity to boost profits with a new factory or two; or a takeover of another firm; or just to pay down a dangerous amount of debt. It will also tell you about the timetable, when you have to send your cheque, when the shares will be credited to you.

To make sure that the company is not doing anything that will harm your interests, the regulator (the UKLA, part of the Financial Conduct Authority – see Chapter 18) will examine the prospectus before it is sent to you. It can take two or three months to go through the regulatory and legal processes.

Pre-emption rights

The UK has particularly strong traditions and laws concerning *pre-emption rights*. These require a company raising new equity capital by selling shares to offer those shares to the existing shareholders first. The owners of the company are entitled to subscribe for the new shares in proportion to their existing holding. This will enable them to maintain their existing percentage ownership of the company – the only difference is that each slice of the company cake is bigger because it has more financial resources under its control.

The shares are usually offered at a significantly discounted price from the market value of the current shares – typically 10–20%. This gives the illusion that shareholders are getting a bargain. But, as we shall see, the benefit from the discount given is taken away by a decline in value of the old shares.

Shareholders can either buy these shares themselves or sell the 'right' to buy to another investor. For further reassurance that the firm will raise the anticipated finance, rights issues are usually underwritten by financial institutions (see Chapter 14 for underwriting).

You will be sent a Provisional Allotment Letter (PAL), which is a temporary document of title showing you the number of new shares you can apply for. To accept, you simply fill in and return the PAL with a cheque or banker's draft for the full amount within the 10 business days allotted.

Illustration of a rights issue

Imagine you own shares in Topup plc. It has 200 million shares in issue. It wants to raise £100m for expansion but does not want to borrow it. Given that its existing shares are quoted on the stock market at 240p, the new rights shares will have to be issued at a lower price to appeal to shareholders because there is a risk of the market share price falling in the period between the announcement and the purchasing of new shares. The problem is that when you get the prospectus and the offer from the company to buy more shares you have at least two weeks (10 working days) to respond. The company sets the price before it sends the prospectus out and there is a risk for you that the market price will move downward below the price you are being asked to hand over for more shares. If this happened in those two weeks you would logically refuse to pay the company for the new shares because old ones can be bought more cheaply in the market.

Topup has decided that the £100m will be obtained by issuing 50 million shares at 200p each. Thus the ratio of new shares to old is 50:200. In other words, this issue is a 'one-for-four' rights issue. Each shareholder will be offered one new share for every four already held. The discount on these new shares is 40p or 16.7% of 240p.

How much will the shares sell for afterward?

If the market price before the issue is 240p, valuing the entire company at £480m and another £100m is pumped into the company by selling 50 million shares at £2, it logically follows that the market price after the rights issue cannot remain at 240p (assuming all else is equal).

A company that was previously valued at £480m which then adds £100m of value to itself (in the form of cash) should be worth

£580m. This company now has 250 million shares, therefore each share is worth £2.32 (i.e. £580m divided by 250 million shares).

An alternative way of calculating the *ex-rights* price is as follows:

four existing shares at a price of 240p	960p
one new share for cash at 200p	200p
value of five shares	1160p
value of one share ex-rights = 1160 ÷ 5	232p

Investors call this the theoretical ex-rights price, TERP.

As a shareholder you have experienced a decline in the price of your old shares from 240p to 232p. A fall of this magnitude necessarily follows from the introduction of new shares at a discounted price. This does not look too good for you, your shares have fallen in price! – but it is OK, you gain value elsewhere.

Value in new shares

The loss on the old shares is exactly offset by the gain in share value on the new rights issue shares. They cost 200p but have a market price of 232p. Let's assume you hold 1000 shares worth £2,400 prior to the rights announcement. You lose £80 on the old shares – their value is now £2,320.

However, you make a gain of £80 on the new shares:

cost of rights shares (250 × £2)	£500
ex-rights value (250 × £2.32)	£580
gain	£80

The company is now a bigger entity. If the directors are correct in thinking that this new money will generate high shareholder returns, you should find that dividends and the share price will rise much higher in the future than it would have done without the rights issue.

Nonsense spoken about the discounted price

When journalists talk glibly of a rights offer being 'very attractively priced for shareholders' they are generally talking nonsense. Whatever the size of the discount the same value will be removed from the old shares to leave the shareholder no worse or better off. Logically, value cannot be handed over to the shareholders from the size of the discount decision.

Shareholders own all the company's shares before and after the rights issue – they can't hand value to themselves without also taking value from themselves. Of course, if the prospects for the company's profits rise because it can now make brilliant capital expenditures, which lead to dominant market positions, then the value of shares will rise – for both the old and the new shares. But this is value creation that has nothing to do with the level of the discount.

What if you do not want to take up the rights?

As owners of the firm, all shareholders must be treated in the same way. To make sure that some shareholders do not lose out because they are unwilling or unable to buy more shares, the law requires that shareholders have a third choice, other than to buy or not buy the new shares. This is to sell the rights on to someone else on the stock market – *selling the rights nil paid*.

Let's assume that you are going through hard times and cannot find the necessary £500. You could sell the rights to subscribe for the shares to another investor and not have to go through the process of taking up any of the shares yourself. Indeed, so deeply enshrined are pre-emption rights that even if you do nothing (perhaps you are sunning yourself on the island you bought by selling some of your successful investments) the company will sell your rights to the new shares on your behalf and send the proceeds to you. (Another possibility is for you to sell some of the rights to provide finance to purchase the remainder – called *'swallowing the tail'*.)

Thus, you would benefit to the extent of 32p per share or a total of £80 (if the market price stays constant), which adequately compensates for the loss on the 1000 shares you hold. But the extent of your control over the company has been reduced – your percentage share of the votes has decreased.

Ex-rights and cum-rights

Old shares bought in the stock market and designated *cum-rights* carry with them the right to subscribe for the new shares in the rights issue. After a cut-off date the old shares go *ex-rights*, which means that any purchaser of old shares during that period will not have the right to purchase any new shares in the rights issue – they remain with the former shareholder.

The price discount decision

It does not matter greatly whether Topup raises £100m on a one-for-four basis at 200p or on a one-for-three basis at 150p per share, or on some other basis. As Table 15.1 shows, whatever the basis of the rights issue, the company will receive £100m and the shareholders will see the price of their old shares decrease, but this will be exactly offset by the value of the rights on the new shares.

Table 15.1 Different rights basis for Topup

Rights basis	Number of new shares	Price of new shares	Total raised
1 for 4	50m	200p	£100m
1 for 3	66.7m	150p	£100m
1 for 2	100m	100p	£100m
1 for 1	200m	50p	£100m

If Topup chose the one-for-one basis this would be regarded as a *deep-discounted rights issue* (current share price 240p, new shares sold at 50p). With an issue of this sort there is only a minute probability that the market price will fall below the rights offer price and therefore there is almost complete certainty that the offer will be taken up.

It seems reasonable to suggest that the underwriting service provided by the institutions is largely redundant here and the firm can make a significant saving. Yet most rights issues are under-written, sometimes involving 100 sub-underwriters.

Other equity issues

Some companies argue that the lengthy procedures and expense associated with rights issues (e.g. the time and trouble it takes to get a prospectus prepared and approved by the UKLA) frustrate directors' efforts to take advantage of oppor-tunities in a timely fashion. Firms in the USA and some other countries have much more freedom to bypass pre-emption rights. They are able to sell blocks of shares to securities houses for distribution elsewhere in the market. This is fast and has low transaction costs.

If this were permitted in the UK there would be a concern for existing shareholders: they could experience a dilution of their voting power and/or the share could be sold at such a low price that a portion of the firm is handed over to new shareholders too cheaply. The UK authorities have produced a compromise under which firms must obtain shareholders' approval through a *special resolution* (a majority of 75% of those voting) at the company's AGM, or at an EGM, to waive the pre-emption right.

Even then the shares must not be sold to outside investors at more than a 5, 7.5 or 10% discount to the share price. While the maximum discount for Main Market companies under the listing rules is 10% (does not apply to AIM and PLUS-market companies) the Association of British Insurers, ABI (representing major investors) guidelines are for a maximum of 5% for placings (see below) and 7.5% for open offers (see below).

This is an important condition. It does not make any difference to existing shareholders if new shares are offered at a deep discount to the market price as long as they are offered to them. If external investors get a discount there is a transfer of value from the current shareholders to the new.

Placings and open offers

In *placings*, new shares of companies already listed are sold directly to a narrow group of external investors. The brokers handling the issue phone round the investment institutions to find buyers. This is cheaper and faster than a rights issue, which requires writing to all the shareholders.

The institutions, as existing shareholders, have produced guidelines to prevent abuse, which normally allow a placing of only a small proportion of the company's capital (a maximum of 5% in a single year, and no more than 7.5% is to be added to the company's equity capital over a rolling three-year period) in the absence of a clawback. Companies can ask to go beyond these limits if they give appropriate justification, but this is rare.

Placings are usually structured so that a prospectus is not required, so this saves money. Also, they can be completed in a matter of days rather than weeks or months for rights issues.

Under *clawback*, existing shareholders have the right to reclaim the placing shares as though they were entitled to them under a rights issue. They can buy them at the price they were offered to the external investors. With a clawback the issue becomes an *open offer*. The major difference compared with a rights issue is that if they do not exercise this clawback right they receive no compensation for any reduction in the price of their existing shares – there are no nil-paid rights to sell.

Vendor placing

If a company wishes to pay for an asset such as a subsidiary of another firm or an entire company with newly issued shares, but the vendor does not want to hold the shares, the purchaser could arrange for the new shares to be bought by institutional investors for cash. In this way the buyer gets the asset, the vendor (e.g. shareholders in the target company in a merger or takeover) receives cash and the institutional investor makes an investment. There is usually a clawback arrangement for a vendor placing. Again, the price discount can be no more than 5, 7.5 or 10% of the current share price.

Acquisition for shares

Shares are often issued in exchange for business assets or shares in another business. While these issues are subject to shareholder approval, the ABI size restrictions are less onerous.

Bought deal

Instead of selling shares to investors, companies are sometimes able to make an arrangement with a securities house whereby it buys all the shares being offered for cash. The securities house then sells the shares on to investors included in its distribution network, hoping to make a profit on the deal. Securities houses often compete to buy a package of shares from the company, with the highest bidder winning. The securities houses take the risk of being unable to sell the shares for at least the amount that they paid. Bought deals are limited by the 5 or 10% pre-emption rules.

Scrip issues

Scrip issues do not raise new money: a company simply gives shareholders more shares in proportion to their existing holdings. The value of each shareholding does not change, because the share price drops in proportion to the additional shares.

They are also known as *capitalisation issues* or *bonus issues*. The purpose is to make shares more attractive by bringing down the price. British investors are thought to consider a share price of £10 and above as less attractive than one in single figures (we are not sure why – researchers fall back on 'it's psychological'). So a company with shares trading at £15 on the market might distribute two 'free' shares for every one held – a two-for-one scrip issue. Since the amount of money in the firm and its economic potential are constant, the share price will theoretically fall to £5.*

Scrip issues are often regarded as indicating confidence in future earnings increases. If this new optimism is expressed in the share price, it may not fall as much as theory would suggest. However, many people are sceptical about the benefits of scrips because of the absence of real economic change, especially in light of the transaction costs.

A number of companies have an annual scrip issue while maintaining a constant dividend per share, effectively raising the level of profit distribution. For example, if a company pays a regular dividend of 20p per share but also has a one-for-ten scrip, the annual income will go up by 10%. (A holder of 10 shares who previously received 200p now receives 220p on a holding of 11 shares.) There will be a date set when the scrip issue will apply. If you are on the shareholder register before that date you will get the issue, after it you will not.

Given that most shares are now held in nominee accounts at brokers (see Chapter 5) the chances are that you will not be holding share certificates and therefore the company will not send the new shares through to your home address. Check with your broker to make sure that your nominee account is properly credited with the new shares following the scrip issue.

Scrip dividends

Scrip dividends are slightly different: shareholders are offered a choice between receiving a cash dividend and receiving additional shares. This is more like a rights issue because the shareholders are making a cash sacrifice if they accept the scrip shares. Shareholders are able to add to their holding without paying stockbroker's commission. Companies are able to raise additional equity capital without the expense of a rights issue.

---

* Scrip issues are achieved by taking reserves on the balance sheet and capitalising them. For example, taking £10m from the 'share premium account' or the 'profit and loss reserves' and transferring it to the 'ordinary share capital' account.

Splits and consolidations

A *share split* (stock split) means that the nominal value of each share is reduced in proportion to the increase in the number of shares, so the total book value of shares remains the same. For example, a company may have one million shares in issue with a nominal value of 50p each. It issues a further one million shares to existing shareholders with the nominal value of each share reducing to 25p, but total nominal value remains at £500,000. Of course, the share price will halve – assuming all else is constant. However, not all else is always constant because, as with a scrip issue, a share split often has a psychological effect on shareholders: it is taken as sign of confidence that the company is going to perform well in the future. Therefore, the share price sometimes does not reduce as much as we might expect.

If the share price goes too low, say 15p, companies may decide to pursue *consolidation of shares*. This is the opposite of a split: the number of shares is reduced and the nominal value of each remaining share rises. If the nominal (par) value is 5p the company could consolidate on the basis of five shares for one. A 25p nominal share would replace five 5p nominal shares and the new share would then trade in the market at $5 \times 15p = 75p$ (or slightly more if investors are more attracted to shares within a 'normal' price range).

Royal Bank of Scotland did this over the Diamond Jubilee weekend in 2012. Shareholders were given one new share for every ten they previously owned. On the Friday they were trading at just under 20p and the next trading day (Wednesday) they were at 200p. Giving its reasons for the share consolidation, RBS said: 'The group currently has a very large number of ordinary shares in issue. This means that a small movement in the share price can result in large percentage movements and considerable volatility in the group's shares.'

16

Stock market indices

Life is like the stock market. Some days you're up. Some days you're down.
And some days you feel like something the bull left behind.

Paul Wall

Once you get into investing you become very interested in those small items tacked onto radio and TV news programmes telling you whether the market is up or down.

'How is the Footsie doing today?' you might ask; or 'Is the Dow having a good day?'

Even though we are long-term investors, and we know that day to day movements are not very relevant to anything, we can't help ourselves. We do mental calculations: 'ooh, up about 1% today, that about £1,000 I've made!' Over longer periods, you may look at how much you have made over six months or a year with your share selection, and then feel pretty smug if you are up 15% when the market has risen by 'only' 12%.

We like to know how the broader market is doing. This is measured by indices. Some of these measure the whole market, whereas others concentrate on particular areas, such as telecom shares or small companies.

How are indices calculated?

A market index is simply an aggregate value of a group of shares tracked over time. But the way in which these are calculated varies; you can do the aggregating in different ways.

The Dow Jones

The first index, the Dow Jones Industrial Average (DJIA, the Dow), was created over 100 years ago. Charles Henry Dow gathered together the prices of 12 large US shares and simply averaged the prices (the statistic was published in the *Wall Street Journal*).

If one company in that list had a market capitalisation 20 times greater than another, that was ignored – it was purely based on share price. Later, the metric was expanded so that now 30 shares are included in the Dow. To be precise, we should say that the Dow is not an index at all, but an average, but people tend not to be so pedantic.

Price weighted versus market-value weighted index (market-cap weighted)

There are difficulties with using only prices to represent the market, *a price-weighted index*. As an example, imagine the simple case of an index consisting of two companies. Farmbrough plc and Nunn plc. Farmbrough is priced at £3 per share and Nunn is priced at £6 per share. In a price-weighted average Nunn takes a greater proportion of the index – two-thirds, in fact.

Thus, if the index starts at £4.50 and the next day the price of Farmbrough rises by 40% to £4.20 while the price of Nunn rises by 10% to £6.60 the overall index moves from £4.50 to £5.40. This is a 20% rise (the opening average price was £3 × 0.5 + £6 × 0.5 = £4.50. The closing average is £4.20 × 0.5 + £6.60 × 0.5 = £5.40).

However, if it is Farmbrough that rises by 10% and Nunn that rises by 40% we see a much bigger jump in the index: Farmbrough is now at £3.30 and Nunn is at £8.40, moving the price-weighted average to £5.85 (that is £3.30 × 0.5 + £8.40 × 0.5). The 'market' has moved up by a greater percentage (30%) simply because the larger weighted share had the bigger move.

It occurred to index compilers that a more representative method is to weight according to the size of the company. Thus a 10% movement in the share price of a large company has a greater effect on an index than a 10% change in a small company's share price.

If we now know that Farmbrough has 1000 million shares in issue, but Nunn has only 50 million shares held by shareholders, the market capitalisations are 1000m × £3 = £3,000m for Farmbrough and 50m × £6 = £300m for Nunn. For a market capitalisation-weighted index Farmbrough will represent 90.9% of the index, whereas Nunn will contribute only 9.1%.

So, if we go back to a 10% rise in the price of Farmbrough and a 40% rise for Nunn, the market-cap weighted index rises by only 12.7%, being dominated by the larger company (that is 10% × 0.909 + 40% × 0.091 = 12.7%). If Nunn had the larger capitalisation then the rise in the index would be much nearly to 40%.

Most modern indices are market-cap weighted so that companies such as Shell or Vodafone have much greater influence on the index than, say, a medium-sized engineering company with a tenth of their market capitalisation.

Notice that we have only allowed for share price changes, ignoring dividends. The main indices discussed below tend to be calculated both as market-capitalisation weighted price change only indices, and as 'total return' versions, which include dividend returns as well.

But most charts you will see, and news broadcasts, concentrate on the version that leaves out the dividends. This does not make much difference over a short period; but when comparing performances over many years you must include the dividends. Certainly, over the 12 years to 2012 when share prices went nowhere we get a distorted view of the returns on shares if we exclude the dividends (around 3–4% per year – over 12 years that adds up).

The major UK market indices

UK – larger companies

The *Financial Times* (FT) joined forces with the Stock Exchange (SE) to create FTSE International in 1995, which has taken over the calculation (in conjunction with the Faculty and Institute of Actuaries) of a number of equity indices. Although most people are only familiar with the FTSE 100, the FTSE also produce a phenomenal 120,000 indices, ranging from country indices (e.g. Indonesia) to football club indices. You will be relieved to hear that I will not describe them all, just concentrate on the most important.

FTSE 100

The Footsie® index is based on the 100 largest companies (generally with over £2bn market capitalisation) which make up approximately 80% of the total market capitalisation of the LSE.* It is a market capitalisation-weighted index. This index has risen fivefold since it was introduced at the beginning of 1984 at a value of 1,000. This is the measure most watched by investors. It is calculated in real time and so changes can observed throughout the day – see free websites.

Market capitalisation of the companies generally ranges from around £2bn to £100bn. The top 10 companies constitute 46% of the index, so if these giant companies are moving in price the whole index is greatly affected. This was shown with a vengeance in 2008 when the index was dominated by large banks such as HSBC (still the biggest in the FTSE 100), RBS and Barclays. Their collapse dragged the index down. It is now dominated by natural resource firms such as BP, Shell, Rio Tinto, BHP Billiton. Also in the top 10 are GlaxoSmithKline, British American Tobacco and BG.

Figure 16.1 shows the constituents of the Footsie in October 2012. Note that as some companies lose market value they may be

---

* Large and relatively safe companies are referred to as *blue chips*.

FTSE 100 SUMMARY

FTSE 100	Closing price	Day's change	FTSE 100	Closing price	Day's change
Aberdeen AM	322	+2.80	Legal & General	136	+1.60
Admiral Group	£10.80	+0.15	Lloyds Banking G	37.81	-0.22
Aggreko	£23.70	+0.23	Marks & Spencer	371.80	+6.30
AMEC	£11.42	+0.02	Meggitt	414.90	+7.20
Anglo American	£18.13	-0.02	Melrose	246.40	+2.40
Antofagasta	£13.22	+0.31	Morrison Supermk	278.20	-2.20
ARM Holdings	598.50	+9	National Grid	699	+1
ABF	£13.28	+0.07	Next	£35.64	-0.28
AstraZeneca	£29.19	+0.08	Old Mutual	172.40	-4.70
Aviva	330	+3.10	Pearson	£12.55	+0.03
Babcock International	964.50	+8.50	Pennon	731	-1.50
BAE Systems	328.10	-5.30	Petrofac	£15.98	-
Barclays	227.85	+5.30	Polymetal Int.	£11.49	+0.14
BG Group	£13.01	-0.15	Prudential	851	+16.50
BHP Billiton	£19.30	+0.17	Randgold Resourc	£77.75	+0.20
BP	436.75	+2.55	Reckitt Benckise	£36.42	+0.25
Brit Am Tobacco	£33.10	+0.10	Reed Elsevier	609.50	+5.50
British Land	521.50	-	Resolution	222.60	+3.70
B Sky B	766.50	+5.50	Rexam	456.50	+16
BT Group	234	+2.40	Rio Tinto	£29.87	+0.64
Bunzl	£11.37	+0.13	Rolls-Royce Hldgs	882	+13
Burberry Group	£10.28	+0.28	Royal Bank Scot	263.50	+3.70
Capita	776.50	+6	Royal Dutch Shel A	£21.69	+0.22
Capital Shop Cntrs.	339.60	+3.30	Royal Dutch Shel B	£22.19	+0.19
Carnival	£23.60	+0.10	RSA Insurance	113.50	+0.50
Centrica	334	+2.50	SABMiller	£27.59	+0.09
Compass Group	693.50	+7	Sage Group	313.70	-0.60
CRH	£12.10	+0.35	Sainsbury	353.20	+1.80
Croda Intl	£23.63	-0.17	Schroders	£15.41	+0.05
Diageo	£17.97	+0.02	Serco Group	600.50	+3.50
ENRC	333.30	+18.60	Severn Trent	£16.89	+0.07
EVRAZ	254.10	+9	Shire	£18.25	+0.05
Experian	£10.72	+0.16	Smith & Nephew	680	-5
Fresnillo	£19.67	+0.38	Smiths Group	£10.74	+0.19
GKN	226.30	+4.30	SSE	£14.35	+0.14
GlaxoSmithKline	£14.65	+0.02	Standrd Chartrd	£14.25	+0.17
Glencore	335.60	-0.90	Standard Life	283.80	+3.40
G4S	268.50	+4.20	Tate & Lyle	688.50	+1.50
Hammerson	467.50	+7.40	Tesco	315.35	-2.80
Hargreaves Lansdown	666	+16.50	Tullow Oil	£14.39	+0.19
HSBC	599.80	+7	Unilever	£23.20	+0.21
IAG	166	+3.50	United Utilities	728.50	-7.50
IMI	971	+20	Vedanta Resource	£11.01	+0.36
Imperial Tobacco	£23.70	+0.27	Vodafone Group	180.65	+2.65
Intercont Hotels	£16.66	-0.03	Weir Group	£18.52	+0.52
Intertek Group	£27.41	+0.17	Whitbread	£24	+0.49
ITV	92.55	+0.60	Wolseley	£27.02	-0.21
Johnson Matthey	£23.39	-0.30	Wood Group (John)	833.50	+22.50
Kazakhmys	738	+31.50	WPP	878	+18.50
Kingfisher	270.30	+1.60	Xstrata	953.50	+5.20
Land Secs Group	775	+4			

Source: ThomsonReuters

Figure 16.1 The list of FTSE 100 companies in *The Financial Times*

Source: The Financial Times Friday 5 October, 2012

overtaken by fast growing ones and so the list of the largest 100 changes regularly. To keep up with this, the FTSE reviews if it is necessary to take companies out and place others into the index every three months (they are not so strict as to remove and replace the moment a share falls below the top 100 capitalisation – that would be too disruptive – there is some judgement and watching along the way, to see if the fall is temporary. Thus, technically, the index is not purely the largest 100 because at the threshold it takes time to promote or demote companies in the index).

For the first 16 years of its life the FTSE 100 zoomed away: these were great times for investors. The period following the dotcom crash of 2000 was a less blessed period with some big ups and downs – see Figure 16.2.

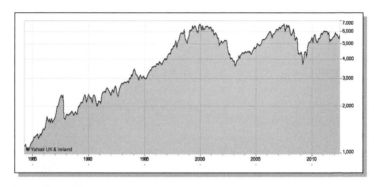

Figure 16.2 The progress of the FTSE 100 index

Source: Yahoo! Finance UK

When judging your portfolio performance it is important to compare like with like. Thus, if you do not have any (or not many) top 100 companies, instead prefering to operate in the mid cap (middle-sized capitalisation firms), then the next index is probably the one for you to compare with. You can do this easily on free websites which will take your portfolio performance over the past few years and place it on a chart alongside a graph of the FTSE 250 index (or other indices you choose).

FTSE 250

No, it is not the top 250. It is based on the largest 250 firms which are in the next size range after the top 100, representing 15–18% of the UK market capitalisation. Capitalisations are generally between £80m and £2bn.

FTSE All-Share

This index is the most representative in that it reflects the average movements of about 600 shares accounting for 98% of the value of the London market. Note: not 'All' the shares are included, merely about 60% of those on the Main Market, but these cover almost all the market capitalisation.

This index is broken down into a number of commercial and industrial sectors, so that investors and companies can use sector-specific yardsticks, such as those for mining or chemicals. Because it is market-cap weighted, the top 10 companies account for over 38% of the weight.

Companies in the FTSE All-Share usually have market capitalisation above £40 million (roughly). It is an aggregation of the FTSE 100, FTSE 250 and the FTSE SmallCap (see below).

FTSE 350

This index is based on the largest 350 quoted companies. It combines the FTSE 100 and the FTSE 250. This cohort of shares is also split into two to give high and low dividend yield groups.

UK – smaller companies

Outside the court of the big boys, there are over 1,700 smaller companies on the LSE (Main Market plus AIM). Despite having small market capitalisations, they can be real bargains. Indeed, many private investors concentrate almost exclusively on the small cap firms. This can be the nurturing ground for the next generation of rapidly growing firms that will eventually take over at the top.

FTSE SmallCap

This index covers listed companies included in the FTSE All-Share but excluded from the FTSE 350, with a market capitalisation of between about £40m and £300m.

FTSE Fledgling

This includes companies listed on the Main Market but too small to be in the FTSE All-Share index.

FTSE AIM All-Share

Index of all AIM companies, excluding those with low liquidity and a low free-float (proportion of a company's shares which are available for trading rather than shares which are unlikely to be sold, such as those in the hands of founders or dominant shareholders).

FTSE All-Small

Combines companies in the FTSE SmallCap with those in the FTSE Fledgling.

Venturing abroad – international indices

USA

S&P 500

The Standard and Poors 500 index tracks the performance of the US's 500 leading companies, and so is more representative of US shares than the 30-share Dow. This covers firms listed on Nasdaq (see below), such as Microsoft and Apple, as well as those on the NYSE, capturing 75% of the value of US quoted shares. The index was first published in 1957.

Professional investors pay more attention to this index rather than the deeply flawed Dow – the news broadcasters are yet to catch up. The top ten companies account for 21% of the index and include Exxon Mobil, IBM, GEC, AT&T, Chevron, Johnson & Johnson, Coca Cola and Wells Fargo, as well as the two computer giants.

NASDAQ Composite

The NASDAQ† market was started as an alternative trading venue to the NYSE in 1971. It is now the second largest exchange in the world. It tends to attract a greater proportion of hi-tech companies. The composite index covers around 3,000 companies and contains companies from many industrial sectors, but its greatest components are the technology, telecoms and internet companies (e.g. Facebook). It is market-cap weighted.

Table 16.1 Important stock market indices

UK indices	Non-UK indices	
FTSE 100	NASDAQ Comp	US
FTSE 250	Dow Jones Ind.	US
FTSE 350	S&P 500	US
FTSE All-Share	FTSE MIB	Italy
FTSE AIM All-Share	Xetra DAX	Germany
FTSE SmallCap	Euro Stoxx 50	Eurozone
FTSE All-Small	CAC 40	France
	AEX	Netherlands
	BEL20	Belgium
	PSI General	Portugal
	Nikkei 225	Tokyo
	Hang Seng	Hong Kong
	BSE Sens	India
	Bovespa	Brazil
	FTSE Straits Times	Singapore
	Shanghai A	China
	ASX All Ordinaries	Australia
	IBEX 35	Spain
	FTSEEurofirst300	Europe
	FTSE All World	World

Source: London Stock Exchange

† Originally it stood for National Association of Securities Dealers Automated Quotations, but now it is NASDAQ in its own right.

NASDAQ 100

Tracks the largest 100 companies on the NASDAQ – this really does have a bias towards hi-tech, e.g. Amazon, Dell and Google.

JAPAN – Nikkei 225

Japan is home to one of the world's best known indices, the Nikkei 225. The Nikkei was established in September 1950. It is one of the few price-weighted indices, comprising 225 of the leading companies of the Tokyo Stock Exchange.

Other important indices

There are many other agencies calculating indices all over the world. The main benchmarks are shown in Table 16.1.

chapter

17

Taxation

If the Lord loveth a cheerful giver, how he must hate the taxpayer!

John Andrew Holmes

You will have to pay tax on your investments. But this does not mean that there aren't ways of legally minimising the amount that you pay. I advise you to take these steps. This chapter explains the forms of tax that have to be paid and the legal ways to reduce the amount.

First, understand the difference between evasion and avoidance of tax. It is illegal to *evade* tax (i.e. deliberately make a false statement or omit a relevant fact) so you need to keep careful records and declare gains at the appropriate time (e.g. on an annual self-assessment tax return).

There are many ways of *avoiding* tax – 'avoiding' is OK, it's legal. You can take advantage of various tax breaks introduced by government – usually to encourage people to act in particular ways (e.g. to save more, or to buy shares in companies just starting up). Thus, there are 'tax-efficient' actions that investors can take to reduce the size of the cheque sent to Her Majesty's Revenue and Customs, HMRC. Be careful though: some of these tax wrappers and other structures can cost more than they are worth. In other words, don't let the tax tail wag the investment dog.

Tax rules and allowances change from year to year. The material below is informed by the 2012–13 tax year rules. HMRC's website (*www.hmrc.gov.uk*) can be useful for keeping you up to date and the Directgov website has some easy-to-follow web pages (*www.direct. gov.uk*).

Stamp duty

A tax payable regardless of whether or not you are a successful investor is stamp duty. A charge of 0.5% of the value of share purchases is levied at the time of purchase. The tax is automatically added to the bill that you receive from your broker.

Some people get quite hot under the collar about stamp duty, saying that it discourages investment in UK shares, is unfair because it is not based on income, eats into pensions and makes the cost of raising equity capital greater for companies. The government raises around £3–4bn per year from it and has shown little interest in abolishing it.

Tax on dividends

Dividends are subject to income tax. When the company sends you a dividend it has already deducted 10% for taxes – you simply receive the net amount after tax.* Unfortunately, if you are not a taxpayer you are unable to reclaim the tax paid. If you are a standard rate tax payer (20% tax rate) you will have no further tax to pay on the dividend.

If you are a higher rate taxpayer (40% marginal rate) you will be chargeable for tax on dividends at 32.5%. Because 10% has already been paid you will have to pay the difference, i.e. 22.5%, at a later date (after completing your tax return).

You will receive a voucher with the dividend payment showing the tax paid. Hold on to the voucher because you will be asked

---

* The 10% tax paid on dividends is counted as part of the company's corporation tax paid for the year.

to declare dividend income and tax payments made on your tax return. It is your responsibility to contact HMRC if you believe you have taxable income (or gains) to declare.

Example

Justin Woolf receives a dividend of 10p per share on his 1,000 shares, a total of £100. He also receives a tax credit for 10% of the gross amount of the dividend amounting to £11.11 (paid by the company on his behalf). This represents 10% of the gross dividend which is £111.11, i.e. £100 + £11.11 = £111.11.

Justin is a higher rate taxpayer and will have to pay tax of 32.5% of the gross dividend: £111.11 × 0.325 = £36.11. He is deemed to have paid £11.11 of this already (the company did it on his behalf) so he has to pay a further £25. Justin therefore walks away with £75.

Capital gains tax (CGT)

If you sell an asset for more than it cost, you may be liable for capital gains tax (CGT). However, you will not be liable for tax on all the difference between the purchase price and the sale value.

- For a start you can deduct various expenses (e.g. stamp duty and brokers' fees).
- Second, against the gain you can set capital losses on other assets made in the same year (or carried forward from an earlier year).
- Third, and perhaps most importantly, you are permitted to make annual gains of £10,600 (in 2012–13) tax free (called an *annual exempt amount*) – so you only pay tax on gains made above this figure.

Basic rate taxpayers pay CGT at 18%, but higher rate taxpayers are charged at 28% on any gains that push them into the higher rate tax bracket when added to income. CGT is worked out for each tax year (which runs from 6 April one year to 5 April the following year). You are required to report gains made on your normal tax return and any tax due must be paid by 31 January after the end of each tax year.

Example

In 2012–13 Adam Treanor has taxable income, after personal allowances, of £26,000. He also makes capital gains on shares bought in 2008, after expenses and offsetting losses, of £17,000.

We deduct his £10,600 annual exempt amount to arrive at the chargeable gain of £6,400. This will be taxed at 18%. Thus £1,152 is payable 31 January 2014.

Tips on reducing CGT

For the majority of private investors the annual allowance of £10,600 will be more than enough to avoid paying any CGT. However, if you are fortunate enough to make substantial gains you might like to know about tax-efficient steps you can take:

- You could *transfer* (sell or give) shares to your spouse or civil partner who could then make use of their annual £10,600 allowance. You have £21,200 of allowance between you. Transfers between spouses and civil partners are not taxed.

- *'Bed and breakfasting'* used to be a very popular way of reducing CGT. If you expected to hold shares for a long time there might be many years when you are not using up the annual CGT allowance. Then, when you do sell, the (say) £50,000 capital gain can be offset against only the final year's allowance – so you face a large tax bill. To get around this, investors would sell shares to realise a capital gain (bed) and then repurchase these the next day (breakfast) in the intervening years. Then the capital gain in the final year is the gain made over merely the last 12 months or so. The loophole is now closed. You now have to leave a gap of 30 days before repurchasing if you wish HMRC to crystallise the capital gain. The exposure to share price change over this month reduced the attractiveness of this technique. The 30-day rule does not apply if you sell the shares and then buy identical shares within an ISA (*'bed-and-ISA'*). Nor does it apply if you sell the shares and then buy identical shares for a SIPP (a *'bed-and-SIPP'*).

■ If your losses in a tax year outweigh your gains, make sure you keep a careful record. You have to let HMRC know that you are offsetting *carry-forward losses* against gains in later years. Note you cannot offset capital losses against income – only against capital gains.

■ If you know you would like to sell out of a company over the next few months, consider the possibility of spreading the gain over two tax years by selling some shares before 5 April and some after that date. Of course, do not take the risk of delay if you think the shares are destined to plunge or you need the cash.

One trick you cannot get away with is to give away the shares or sell them at an artificially low price to an accomplice who then sells them for you. HMRC are on to this one – they will value the disposal at the proper market price for CGT purposes.

Individual savings accounts (ISAs)

Individual savings accounts (ISAs) who are run by financial institutions such as brokers or banks, who will impose charges. They should not be viewed as investments in themselves: they are 'tax wrappers' or 'baskets' which contain the underlying investments. The underlying investments fall into two categories:

■ **Cash.** With a cash ISA your money is placed in deposit accounts (e.g. with banks or building societies) or National Savings products.

■ **Stocks and shares.** This covers shares, collective investments such as unit trusts,† life insurance policies and bonds. AIM shares are excluded because they are not listed and so have their own tax benefits – see later.

---

† See Glen Arnold, *The Financial Times Guide to Investing* (Financial Times, Prentice Hall, 2010).

The tax benefits of ISAs are:

- no capital gains tax to pay on investments held in the ISA;
- tax is not deducted from interest.

Unfortunately, one of the benefits of ISAs has been removed: dividends on shares will be taxable in the normal way for a basic rate taxpayer. That is, the 10% tax paid on dividend income from the company cannot be reclaimed. However, higher rate taxpayers are still exempt from paying additional tax on dividend income from ISA investments – thus saving an amount equal to 22.5% of the gross dividend.

With ISAs you can either put the entire annual limit of £11,280 into an equity ISA, or put £5,640 into a cash ISA and the remainder (£5,640) into stocks and shares. You do not have to invest the full amount all in one go – you can make regular payments or irregular lump sums through the year, just so long as the total does not breach the annual limits. The amount you can put into ISAs each year is not increased if you also withdraw some money in the same tax year. So, if you put £11,280 into a share ISA in November and then withdraw £1,800 in December, you cannot put another £1,800 in that tax year – you have already used your £11,280 allowance for the tax year.

You are permitted to withdraw money from an ISA at any time without incurring a tax charge; however, the ISA provider may impose penalties or restrict your freedom of action (e.g. if you agreed to lock your money into a bank's cash ISA for a year).

Self-select ISA

With a *self-select ISA* you decide which shares, etc. should be bought. You can buy and sell as many shares within the ISA as you like and as often as you like. Not all ISA managers/brokers offer self-select ISAs, so you may have to shop around. Be wary of the charges levied by the providers of self-select ISAs. In addition to dealing charges for buying the shares, an initial charge may be payable, followed by an annual fee linked to the value of the fund (0.5–1.75% per annum) or a flat amount each quarter (say

£12.50). There may also be a charge for dividend collection and reinvestment.

The ISA debate

Many doubt the wisdom of holding share ISAs, especially with the withdrawal of the basic rate tax benefit on dividends. Most private investors are unlikely to be caught by CGT given the £10,600 annual allowance. Buying an equity ISA wrapper for your share investments can therefore mean paying annual management charges of 0.5–1.75% for the minor tax advantage that if you are a higher rate taxpayer you will pay a maximum of 10% on dividend income. If dividend income is around 4% of the value of your holding, saving 22.5% of that (i.e. 0.9%) will often be outweighed by the management charges.

On the other hand, many people have now become 'ISA millionaires'; by putting in the maximum allowed each year and through wise investing they now have over £1m in their ISAs. For these people, there is a fairly high likelihood that they will make capital gains of over £10,600 in most years; a few share sales in takeovers plus a few sales due to profit-taking can easily add up to a large CGT bill.

Even if you have managed to put away 'only' £100,000 or so into your ISA you will start to notice the benefits of the CGT shelter. It is perfectly possible for one or two of your shares to produce gains of over £10,600. Selling them outside of an ISA can result in painful 18% or 28% tax. This may make you more reluctant to sell overpriced shares compared with if they were in a tax wrapper.

Personal pensions

Personal pensions are very tax-efficient if you are saving/investing for the long term:

■ The money you put in (your contributions) qualify for full tax relief. This means that if you contribute, say, £2,880 from taxed earnings the government then adds back tax (at 20%) to the fund amounting to £720, meaning that £3,600 is added to your pension pot. Higher rate taxpayers get additional tax relief – they claim back the other 20% of tax paid when they fill in their annual tax returns.

▓ Once the money is in the fund it can grow without tax being levied on interest income, or on capital gains (however, dividend income is taxed).

▓ When you reach retirement you can take 25% of the fund in cash, tax-free. The rest has to be put into a fund that will provide you with an *annuity* – regular payments for the rest of your life. These are provided by insurance companies. *Income drawdown* ('unsecured pension') is an alternative to an annuity – consult a specialist book/website, e.g. *www. pensionsadvisoryservice.org.uk/*. Income drawdown allows people to draw an income from the pension fund and invest the rest as they choose, e.g. in the stock market. This income is taxable.

You are permitted to start receiving the pension after the age of 55. Opening a number of schemes allows you to begin drawing benefits at different points. You do not have to stop work to start receiving benefits under these schemes.

There is a wide range of type of funds: e.g. shares (UK or overseas), bonds and cash. You can put money into a fund that invests in a mixture of securities. You can save a regular amount into a personal pension (the minimum is usually £20 a month) or pay in lump sums on an *ad hoc* basis.

A major disadvantage with personal pensions as investment vehicles is that you cannot get your money back quickly – at least not until you are 55. Even when you start to make use of the savings you are compelled to leave most of the money (75%) in the fund rather than having the flexibility to do what you wish with it.

Self-invested personal pensions (SIPPs)

A disadvantage of standard personal pensions is that you have no choice over the specific investments held in the fund – this is left up to the fund manager. If you are confident about your share selection capabilities then you may like to opt for a self-invested personal pension (SIPP). These allow you to instruct the fund administrator to buy and sell shares and other investments on your behalf within the SIPP wrapper. You gain the same tax advantages as for a standard personal pension and you have control over the investment performance. The disadvantage is that you are likely to pay more in charges.

- Because of increased competition you can now start a SIPP with a commitment of only £50 per month or a minimum lump sum of £1,000.

- The charging structure varies enormously. Some SIPP providers do not levy an initial charge (this can be up to £500) for putting money into the fund (a *set-up charge*) but then charge an annual fee of about 0.5–1.5%, with a minimum of between £100 and £400 per year. Other providers will charge you £200–£500 for setting up the account followed by fixed annual fees of £200–£300. Each deal buying or selling securities within the fund would also be subject to brokers' fees of £10–£30.

- The lower cost SIPPs tend to limit the range of investments you can buy to shares, collective investments (e.g. unit trusts) and cash, rather than allow you to invest in more exotic assets such as property. With these the set up cost may be £100 or less, with an annual fee of 0.5%.

- You can opt for advisory or discretionary SIPP funds, where a broker would either give advice on investments or take responsibility for making investment decisions. These accounts are more expensive than execution-only.

- The rule that 25% of a pension pot can be taken as cash-free lump sum applies to SIPPs as well.

- SIPPs can be taken out for a non-tax-paying relative – HMRC will top up the fund at the basic rate of tax. The limit for this is a grossed-up £3,600 per year – so you would put in a maximum of £2,880.

Warnings on pensions

- Be careful that you don't lose half of your fund in management charges of one sort or another. Look very carefully at the small print.

- Don't trade frequently. You are likely to lose a tremendous amount in dealing costs for little gain.

- Providers can, and sometimes do, introduce new charges on SIPPs.

- Make sure that it is relatively cheap and painless to transfer your pension to another provider if the service is poor.

- Interest rates on cash balances held by a SIPP provider may be low. Shop around and ask before you sign up. Any cash deposited with a SIPP provider is protected under the Financial Services Compensation Scheme (see Chapter 18).

- When you start to withdraw money from a personal pension this will be subject to income tax.

Tax benefits of investing in AIM companies

First bad news: AIM shares cannot be included in ISAs because they are not 'listed' on the Main Market of the London Stock Exchange.

Now the good news: they are allowed in SIPPs, there are inheritance tax advantages and there are tax benefits in buying them through Venture Capital Trusts (VCTs) and the Enterprise Investment Scheme (EIS).

Inheritance tax

If you owned AIM company shares for more than two years, and these are included in your estate for inheritance tax purposes, you are allowed to pass on the shares free of tax, either during your lifetime or as part of your will.

Venture Capital Trusts (VCTs)

VCTs are quoted companies that gather together a pot of investment money by selling their shares to investors. This pot of money is then used to buy shares in smaller unlisted trading companies. These are mostly small entrepreneurial companies that do not have a stock market quote, but some of them are AIM companies (and PLUS-market companies). The VCT must buy new shares in these companies, i.e. newly issued by the company raising capital, rather than from existing shareholders in the secondary market.

The tax breaks for putting money into VCTs are that

- there is an immediate relief on current year's income at 30% – put £10,000 in and get a tax rebate of £3,000, and
- the returns, income and capital gains, are free of tax.

Individuals claiming tax relief for money put into a VCT are limited to a maximum of £200,000 placed with VCTs per year. Furthermore, these benefits are only available to investors buying new VCT shares, i.e. on launch of the VCT or when a VCT raises new money (not VCT shares bought from other investors in the secondary market) who hold the investment for at least five years. The VCT managers can only invest in companies worth less than £7m.

These trusts offer investors a way of investing in a broad spread of small firms with high potential, but with greater uncertainty, in a tax-efficient manner. They also offer the possibility of being able to sell the VCT shares in the secondary market on the LSE – however, for some VCTs there is little demand and so you may have difficulty selling.

VCTs can have several charges applied including an initial charge, an annual management charge, additional expenses and incentive bonuses to the fund manager. Total fees are around 3.5% per year. Check out five-year return performances of existing VCTs before buying into a new fund.

Enterprise Investment Scheme (EIS)

The EIS is a government initiative to encourage the flow of risk capital to smaller companies. Income tax relief at 30% is available for investments of up to £1,000,000 made directly into qualifying company shares.‡ By putting £10,000 into an EIS qualifying company an investor will pay £3,000 less tax, so the effective cost is only £7,000. There is also CGT relief. No CGT is payable on the disposal of shares in an EIS company after holding for three years (or after three years of commencement of trading, if later). Losses within EIS are allowable against income tax or capital gains. Furthermore, the value of EIS investments is not counted for inheritance tax after only two years.

'Direct investment' means investing when the company issues shares. It does not mean buying shares in the secondary market from other investors. The tax benefits are lost if the investments are held for less than three years. To raise money from this source the firm must have been carrying out a 'qualifying activity' – this generally excludes financial investment and property companies. The company must not be on the Main Market and the most it can raise under the EIS in any one year is usually £5m. The company must not have gross assets worth more than £15m or more than 250 employees.

Be a cheerful giver: get the taxman to give away money too!

Imagine that you have done really well as an investor and are now in the position to be generous to others less fortunate. Then you can give your shares to charity which means that you can take advantage of some tax breaks.

If you give shares, or sell them to a charity at less than their market value, you can claim income tax relief and lower your tax bill, as well as getting CGT relief. Shares allowed under this include those

---

‡ It is also possible to 'carry-back' the investment to the previous tax year – offsetting the invested amount against tax paid then – tax can be reclaimed.

of LSEs Main Market and AIM as well as PLUS and many overseas shares.

If you bought some shares for £10,000 and they are now worth £20,000 you could hand them over to the charity of your choice and then deduct the market value from your normal taxable income. So for 40% taxpayers the charity benefits from the ownership of £20,000 of shares and the giver pays £8,000 less tax that year. If you have made a large capital gain and are therefore expecting to pay CGT, you can give the shares to a charity who will not have to pay the tax – nor will you.

You need to complete a stock transfer form (from the company's registrar) to take the shares out of your name and put them into the charity's name. The charity will then give you a certificate stating that they have acquired them.

When you complete an annual self-assessment tax return, you can make your claim on the form. Alternatively, if you pay tax through PAYE you can write to your tax office with details of your gift or sale to a charity and how much tax relief you would like to claim. HMRC will change your tax code for the current year reducing your monthly tax bill, or give you a refund for an earlier year.

chapter

Regulation of the markets

Fraud and falsehood only dread examination.

Samuel Johnson

Scams

Imagine the scene. You have made a decent amount of money with your investments over the years. You have done your usual morning check on your portfolio and the market. While enjoying your morning coffee you get a call from a very nice-sounding man asking you about your investments and aspirations. He's particularly interested in your triumphs and what sort of size your fund has grown to.

And would you know it, he has an amazing opportunity that you really ought to invest in! But he is too polite to push you there and then to buy. Perhaps he can phone back in a week or two, when you have had time to digest the written material he will kindly email to you. No high pressure there then. Could he really be a conman?

Maybe to make sure you check out some details about the company he said was a sure winner on the internet. It is a relief to find that it does actually exist. And, would you believe it, everything on the website(s) gives a glowing account of its prospects. Message board postings are full of praise.

So what if it is traded on an obscure market in a far away country. That is exactly what your gentleman caller had said. After all that's where the opportunities are: mines in South America, hi-tech in America or new companies in the leading developing countries. That's where the money is! That's where the future lies! Not in old-fashioned boring UK companies that produce pedestrian returns of 10% or so a year.

What did he say? His top-pick forestry company in Indonesia had given its shareholders 120% increases last year, and the year before. Better for you to jump in before everyone else hears about this and the price goes through the roof.

Two weeks later he calls you again. He politely asks you how you are doing, chats about the markets and casually mentions the company again. He is astonished that others in the market have not heard about this one. Don't they know that it is bound to rise at least 100% in the next few months? What's more, because he has got along with you so well he will tell you about a way into this company at an even lower price than other investors. All you need to do is send him a cheque and he'll do the rest. Expect to see your money doubled in no time! Who knows, maybe in a few months he'll have another great opportunity for you. By which time you will have received statements showing the value of your first investment doing very nicely.

But, how much is a statement worth? Can you turn it into cash? 'Ah well ...', says the voice on the other end of the phone '... that may take some time'.

You have been the victim of a *boiler room scam*. They are very convincing, very persuasive and very immoral. They are also annoyingly persistent. As much as £200m is taken off UK investors each year. Many are elderly, who desperately need their savings. I'm always amazed at how apparently sophisticated and experienced investors fall for these scams. Some get so determined to recover the money previously lost that they use credit cards when they have gone through all their cash. While some end up losing their homes, the average loss is £20,000 (but one person lost £6m).

Quite often, the shares do actually exist. It is just that they are traded on illiquid stock markets (if you can call them stock markets) in unsavoury parts of the world or on developed country markets that the locals are very wary of because of the lack of proper regulation to prevent widespread rip-offs. When you come to sell there is no one around willing to buy. Yes, but who sold you the shares in the first place? Well, the scammer of course, or an accomplice, at a highly inflated price. The company may, in reality, be almost worthless, but you have paid a price that would make a Mayfair antique dealer blush.

Alternatively, the company may not have obtained a quotation on a stock market yet. But it will do soon, you know. If you buy now then you get at bargain basement price and multiply your money 2-, 5-, 10-fold when it does float. Of course, it never does. Or if it does it is worth nothing.

The scammers often have a close relationship with the directors of the company being promoted. They operate from overseas, out of the sight and control of the UK regulators and prosecution authorities in places such as Spain, Dubai and South Asia. Quite often they will tell you a blatant lie that they are based in London and regulated by the authorities there. 'Look! You can check the telephone number, and the website, and the company literature.' Definitely London then.

Telephones are not their only tools to trap investors. They also use word of mouth, post, advertise in newspapers and seminars. They may offer you a free research report into a company you already hold shares in, or a free gift or discount on their dealing charges.

Action you can take

- Do not respond to cold-callers. Real stockbrokers and properly regulated financial advisers do not cold-call. Tell the crooks that they are conmen and immoral, and hang up.
- Only deal with financial service firms that are authorised and regulated by UK regulators – see below. You'll have to verify by calling them back on the number on the UK regulator's website (they may use the name of a high reputation/ regulated firm).

- The golden rule for all investments: always understand what you are investing in. Do not be intimidated into being afraid to show your ignorance by asking key questions about the securities you are being asked to buy before you commit. How does the company make money? What are the risks? What are the safeguards?

Another share scam

The fraudster finds out that you own shares in a company. He then offers to buy them from you at a higher price than their market value. 'What is wrong with that?' you ask. He will require money up front as a bond or other form of security. You will get this back if the sale does not go ahead, they say. Of course, you never hear from them again. This one is called an *advanced fee scam*.

UK regulation

These scammers know that the UK authorities are on to them, that is why they operate from abroad. The risks of being defrauded by a UK regulated financial service provider are very much reduced by the quality of the systems developed to protect investors and enhance faith in the finance industry. We now look at the regulatory system which protects against not only fraud but other concerns such as incompetence, ignorance and biased advice.

Let's first think about the sort of things that you might like to reduce the likelihood of harm being done to you as an investor – as you'll see later, these are now covered by UK regulators.

Only authorised people can be allowed to sell to investors

Thus we need some sort of licensing system. Is a person, e.g. a stock broker, 'fit and proper'? This comes down to a judgement of good character and may be informed by past behaviour, e.g. criminal convictions. Only those who have met the standards required (integrity, capability) should be allowed to provide a service in the industry. Training schemes and qualifications are to be encouraged to raise standards.

Continued observance of the organisation by regulators

Disclosure of information about the operations of the financial firm and on-going monitoring may reveal whether a conflict of interest exists, whether risk management procedures are sound, whether the managers are competent and the institution is run with integrity.

Make sure the markets are run fairly

Safeguards need to be in place to ensure that investors are treated fairly.

- There must be a fair treatment of investors and prohibitions on insider dealing, e.g. directors using information which only they have to make a killing buying shares ahead of, say, a takeover or an announcement of bumper profits.
- Market manipulation or abuse must be countered, e.g. the spreading of false rumours to push up (or down) a share is to be outlawed and prosecuted.
- There must be transparency of trading, e.g. open disclosure of price quotes by market makers, and the prices of trades to be published.
- When it comes to new issues of shares there must be a clear and complete prospectus and financial statements (see Chapter 14).

They must be careful with your money

Apart from outright fraud a firm must protect client assets while it holds them on behalf of the client – e.g. ring-fencing them, meaning that they do not mix their money with the broker's money.

They are run safely

You want to be sure that they are not suddenly going to go kaput, letting you down in the middle of an investment strategy or tying up your money in legal wrangling for months. For this reassurance they should not have too much debt or take on too much risk.

Good systems if things go wrong

If you have a complaint you would expect that it will be handled well, that the company will listen to you and try to rectify the problem. If necessary you want to secure recompense.

The bad guys should be punished

In the event of non-compliance with the rules penalties should be imposed, e.g. fines, de-licensing, imprisonment, banning directors from the industry. For less serious offences a private warning or public censure may be sufficient.

The Financial Conduct Authority (FCA)

So, those are the basic requirements from a shareholder's perspective; what have the British authorities done about it? They have created some large and powerful regulators to supervise the system.

Until 2013 the *Financial Services Authority, FSA,* dominated the scene. It was a 'super-regulator' with oversight of an amazing range of financial sectors. In 2013 the FSA split in two. The main body, the *Financial Conduct Authority, FCA,* is now the super-regulator covering a very wide range of financial services – see Figure 18.1. But one important function, that of the individual regulation of the 2,200 biggest brokers, banks and insurers on the issue of whether they are safe and sound (enough cash reserves, low debt, well run, not taking too much risk), is now the task of the *Prudential Regulatory Authority, PRA,* a subsidiary of the Bank of England. It is responsible for granting permission for their activities and approving their senior management.

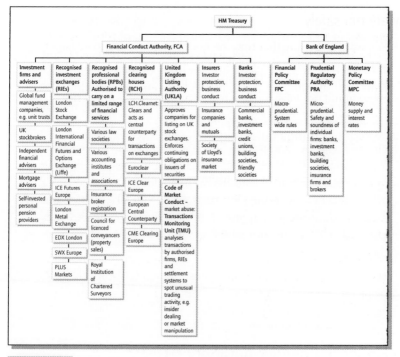

The diagram shows:

HM Treasury

Financial Conduct Authority, FCA | Bank of England

Investment firms and advisers	Recognised investment exchanges (RIEs)	Recognised professional bodies (RPBs) Authorised to carry on a limited range of financial services	Recognised clearing houses (RCH)	United Kingdom Listing Authority (UKLA)	Insurers Investor protection, business conduct	Banks Investor protection, business conduct	Financial Policy Committee FPC	Prudential Regulatory Authority, PRA	Monetary Policy Committee MPC
Global fund management companies, e.g. unit trusts	London Stock Exchange	Various law societies	LCH.Clearnet: Clears and acts as central counterparty for transactions on exchanges	Approves companies for listing on UK stock exchanges. Enforces continuing obligations on issuers of securities	Insurance companies and mutuals	Commercial banks, investment banks, credit unions, building societies, friendly societies	Macro-prudential. System wide rules	Micro-prudential. Safety and soundness of individual firms: banks, investment banks, building societies, insurance firms and brokers	Money supply and interest rates
UK stockbrokers	London International Financial	Various accounting institutes and associations	Euroclear		Society of Lloyd's insurance market				
Independent financial advisers	Futures and Options Exchange (Liffe)		ICE Clear Europe						
Mortgage advisers	ICE Futures Europe	Insurance broker registration	European Central Counterparty	Code of Market Conduct – market abuse: Transactions Monitoring Unit (TMU) analyses transactions by authorised firms, RIEs and settlement systems to spot unusual trading activity, e.g. insider dealing or market manipulation					
Self-invested personal pension providers	London Metal Exchange	Council for licenced conveyancers (property sales)	CME Clearing Europe						
	EDX London	Royal Institution of Chartered Surveyors							
	SWX Europe								
	PLUS Markets								

Figure 18.1 UK financial services industry regulation

The FCA has responsibility for protecting consumers and preserving market integrity, covering:

- investor protection;
- market supervision and regulation;
- business conduct of financial services firms, including the supervision of investment managers;
- civil and criminal enforcement of market abuse rules;
- UK Listing Authority – supervision of initial public offerings and subsequent monitoring of listed companies (see Chapter 14).

The Bank of England has the responsibility of ensuring the safety of the banking system. Its *Financial Policy Committee, FPC,* makes decisions that apply to the entire sector to ensure systemwide financial stability including the avoidance of credit and asset bubbles (*Macroprudential regulation*), e.g. it might set nationwide borrowing limits such as the maximum amount of a loan relative to the value of the property backing up that loan. The PRA division does the hard work of day-to-day handling of individual institutions to ensure firm-level stability and soundness. Of course, the Bank also has the *Monetary Policy Committee, MPC,* to set interest rates and adjust the money supply.

The FCA can be described as semi-detached from government: it is financed by the industries it regulates, but its powers come from legislation; it often consults the financial services companies before deciding on principles, rules and codes of conduct, but it has basic principles approved by the government and it is answerable to the Treasury, which appoints its board and, through them, Parliament.

The FCA's objectives:

1 Maintaining confidence in the financial system.
2 Protecting consumers.
3 Reducing financial crime, such as money laundering, fraud and insider dealing.
4 Financial stability – contributing to the protection and enhancement of stability in the UK financial system.
5 Helping people to gain the knowledge, aptitude and skills to manage their financial affairs effectively by promoting public understanding of the financial system.

While pursuing these objectives, the regulator makes it clear that it is not removing all risk for the investor. Investment risk is an inherent part of the system and those who take the benefits from an investment when everything goes right have to accept that from time to time investment losses will occur. Also, the complete absence of consequences for the client should a financial firm fail may encourage laziness in choosing a place for their money, and so the FCA does not promise to rescue failed firms, nor guarantee all money deposited/invested with them (but see Financial Services Compensation Scheme later).

What the FCA does
Authorisation
All firms or individuals offering financial advice, products or services in the UK must be authorised by the FCA.* Engaging in a regulated activity without authorisation can result in a two-year prison sentence. The FCA insists on high standards when assessing for authorisation. These require competence, financial soundness and fair treatment of customers. Firms are authorised to carry out specific activities, e.g. giving financial advice only, or managing a client's money in a fund, or stockbroking.

Monitoring
Even after initial approval, firms cannot relax as the FCA continues to monitor adequacy of management, financial resources and internal systems and controls. It also insists that any information provided to investors is clear, fair and not misleading. If there is a failure to meet these standards the firms can be fined or even stopped from doing business. The FCA also works closely with the criminal authorities and uses civil and criminal powers.

Principles over law
The FCA emphasises broad principles rather than its rules. The problem with a regulator sticking strictly to rules is that they can result in inflexibility - just 'ticking boxes' - rather than concentrating the minds of the regulated on the spirit underlying the rules. Also a rule-based approach can be less flexible when it comes to permitting innovation from existing or new firms.

A principles-based approach has less prescription and allows the regulator to meet new situations (e.g. new tricks by those smart people in the City) by using some degree of judgement rather than being hidebound by rules. Lawyers will forever be finding loopholes in rules; they find that more difficult if the rules are set

---

* Or have special exemption. A list of those registered as authorised by the FSA is at *www.fsa.gov.uk.*

in a framework of general principles, when the principles have greater weight.

What if you have a complaint?

There are three steps you can take.

Raise the issue with the financial service company

All firms should have a formal complaints procedure, and you are encouraged by the FCA to start here, giving the firm a chance to right the wrong. After all, the firm is best placed to check its records and see what happened. Most regulated firms have *compliance officers* whose job it is to ensure the FCA rules are being followed. Roughly three out of four complainants dissatisfied with the response of the company choose not to pursue it further, believing it would be futile to do so. However, there are further positive steps you could take.

Independent complaints scheme

Most financial services firms belong to an independent complaints scheme – the FCA insists in most cases.† These are beneficial to the system because they increase the confidence of investors and other financial clients by responding to the fear of consumers that they lack knowledge to be able to stand up to the financial professionals. There are two types: arbitration schemes and ombudsman schemes. Under both, the complaint will be investigated and, if found to be justified, the firm will be ordered to put matters right. Many of the schemes provide for a financial award, up to a maximum of £100,000. Under arbitration, both the complainant and the firm agree in advance to accept the arbitrator's decision. Importantly, in accepting this the complainant gives up the right to take the case to court. The advantage is that it is much quicker and cheaper than going to court. Under the *Financial Ombudsman Scheme (FOS)*‡ the independent and impartial ombudsman collects together the facts of the case and arrives at what seems to him/

---

† The firm's literature should set out its regulatory body and scheme.
‡ *www.financial-ombudsman.org.uk* or telephone 0800 023 4567.

her a reasonable and fair settlement. The firm is then under an obligation to accept the decision,§ but the complainant remains free to take the case to court. The service is free to consumers. The ombudsman's approach is less legalistic than arbitration and allows for more 'common-sense' factors of fairness.

If the FOS finds in the complainant's favour it can order a firm to pay compensation up to a maximum of £100,000. The FOS may even order the firm to pay compensation for distress and inconvenience on top of financial loss.

Go to court

Litigation is often expensive, time-consuming and frustrating, and so should only be contemplated as a last resort. A relatively fast and informal service is provided by the small claims track or the small claims court (maximum claim in England and Wales is £5,000, in Northern Ireland and Scotland it is £3,000). The complainant does not need a solicitor, and court fees are low. The complainant may not even have to attend the court as judges can make judgements on the paper evidence.

Compensation

The complaint steps described in the last section are all well and good if the firm that has behaved badly is still in existence. But what if it is defunct? The *Financial Services Compensation Scheme* (*FSCS*)¶ can compensate consumers (and small companies) if an authorised company is unable to pay money it owes. Note that if a consumer does business with a firm not authorised by the FCA, e.g. an offshore company,** he/she is not covered by FSCS or the complaints procedure. The FSCS service is free for the consumer and small business. For investments the maximum payout is £50,000 per person.

---

§ Although they can appeal through the courts.

¶ *www.fscs.org.uk*.

** One based and regulated outside of the UK, such as Bermuda or Jersey.

Regulation of markets

The FCA supervises exchanges, clearing houses and settlement houses. It also conducts market surveillance and monitors transactions on seven *recognised investment exchanges, RIEs*. The RIEs work with the FCA to protect investors and maintain the integrity of markets. Much of the monitoring and enforcement is delegated to the RIEs. The LSE, for example, vets new stockbrokers and tries to ensure compliance with LSE rules, aimed at making sure members (e.g. market makers and brokers) act with the highest standards of integrity, fairness, transparency and efficiency. It monitors market makers' quotations and the price of actual trades to ensure compliance with its dealing rules. It is constantly on the look-out for patterns of trading that deviate from the norm with the aim of catching those misusing information (e.g. insider dealing), creating a false or misleading impression to the disadvantage of other investors or some other market distorting action.

The LSE, in partnership with the FCA, also requires companies to disseminate all information that could significantly affect their share prices. It insists on timely and accurate director statements to the stock market so that there is not a false market in the company's shares.

Regulation of companies

If you invest in a company by buying its shares, you have a right to receive information about that company, and to expect that there are laws and other pressures to discourage the management from going astray and acting against your interests.

There are various checks and balances in the corporate world.

- The most important are the requirements under the *Companies Acts*. The Department for Business, Innovation and Skills enforces the law and is able to intrude into a company's affairs.
- Accountants and auditors also function, to some extent, as regulators, helping to ensure companies do not misrepresent their position.

- Furthermore, any member of the public may access the accounts of any company easily and cheaply at Companies House (*www.companieshouse.gov.uk*).

- The media keep a watchful stance – always ready to reveal stories of fraud, greed or incompetence. A free press has a very important role in ferreting out and reporting foul play, poor service, incompetence and chicanery.

- In the case of mergers of listed or other public limited companies, the *City Panel on Takeovers and Mergers* acts to ensure fairness for all shareholders.

- The *Office of Fair Trading* and the *Competition Commission* investigate, rule on and enforce remedies with regard to anti-competitive behaviour.

- The FCA is one of several UK organisations that investigates and responds to suspicions of fraud. The *City of London Police* is, however, the 'National Lead Force' for fraud with a remit to create a centre of excellence for fraud investigations and to use its expertise to help police forces across the UK. It is particularly concerned with organised crime groups such as boiler room scammers, and securing major convictions.

- The *Serious Fraud Office, SFO,* investigates and prosecutes serious or complex fraud and corruption exceeding £1m in value. It is a part of the criminal justice system, but remains an independent government department (with a high degree of autonomy from political control). If a suspected fraud is likely to give rise to widespread public concern, be complex and thus require specialist knowledge to investigate, or be international in scope, then the SFO is inclined to be the organisation that tackles it.

Be reassured, but take precautions

All in all, criminals and incompetents in UK financial services sectors have an array of agencies tracking them down. This makes the environment for the UK share investors one of the safest in the world. This is not to say that you can never by caught out, so do not put all your money with one organisation. By splitting between a number if one goes bust or becomes rotten you have the others to fall back on. Also, make sure that these organisations are regulated. If you deal with those that are not, even if they are legally operating in the UK, you may have no protection.

Index